Study and Revise

GCSE

Higher Maths

Philip Hooper and Sheila Hunt

KEY TO SYMBOLS

As you read through this book you will notice the following symbols. They will help you find your way around the book more quickly.

 shows you a handy hint to help you learn

 points out a potential hazard that could cause a problem

 explains some of the mathematical jargon that you might meet

 highlights important points to remember

Text © Philip Hooper and Sheila Hunt 2004

First published in this edition 2004
exclusively for WHSmith by
Hodder & Stoughton Educational
338 Euston Road
London NW1 3BH

Impression number   10 9 8 7 6 5 4 3 2
Year   2010 2009 2008 2007 2006 2005

Prepared by Techset Ltd
Printed and bound in the UK by Scotprint

A CIP record for this book is available from the British Library

ISBN 0 340 85862 1

Contents

Contents

This book covers the topics you need to answer those difficult questions on the Higher Maths paper. You do not have to follow this book in any particular order, so you might want to tackle the areas you have most difficulty with first – try not to leave them to last. Not only does this book tell you how to do things, it also tells you what the common pitfalls are and how to avoid them: watch out for the banana skins.

The chapters in the contents list are separated into four subject areas: Number, Algebra, Shape and space, and Handling data. If yours is a modular syllabus, find out the topics being examined for each component, and make sure of them before you take the module. Look at the back of the book for exam-style questions to test yourself before the exam.

What makes this book different? Just look at any chapter at random and you will find all sorts of short cuts, easy methods and original ideas to make learning and remembering maths easier – and, dare we say it, maybe more enjoyable – than you ever thought was possible.

Good luck.

Philip Hooper and Sheila Hunt

PREVIEW

By the end of this chapter you will be able to:

- **identify the different types of numbers**
- **manipulate rational and irrational numbers**
- **simplify numbers involving surds**
- **rationalise the denominator**
- **evaluate an unknown by substituting given values into a formula**
- **approximate and round to the nearest unit**
- **identify the interval in which the value of a rounded figure may fall**
- **simplify expressions involving indices, including negative and fractional indices**
- **express a large or a small number in standard form**
- **convert decimals to fractions and vice versa**
- **express recurring decimals as fractions.**

Whenever you see this sign – take care.

Remember: you have been warned!

Factors, primes and rational numbers

Factors are numbers that 'divide into' other numbers without leaving a remainder.
For example 6 is a factor of 12, 5 is a factor of 40.

Prime numbers can only be divided by themselves and 1. In other words, they have exactly 2 factors, themselves and 1.
Note that 1 is not a prime number.

Prime factors are prime numbers which are factors of another number.
For example 6 is a factor of 12, but 5 is a prime factor of 40.

Reciprocals are the numbers you get by turning another number 'upside-down'. With whole numbers this becomes '1 over' the number.
On a calculator this is the key marked `1/x` or `x⁻¹`.
For example:

$2 = \dfrac{2}{1}$ The reciprocal is $\dfrac{1}{2}$ (or 0.5 on the calculator)

$2.5 = 2\tfrac{1}{2} = \dfrac{5}{2}$ The reciprocal is $\dfrac{2}{5}$ or 0.4

Finding the reciprocal

The reciprocal of x is $\dfrac{1}{x}$ or x^{-1}

The reciprocal of 4 is $\dfrac{1}{4}$

The reciprocal of $\dfrac{5}{9}$ is $\dfrac{9}{5}$

So $\left(\dfrac{4}{9}\right)^{-1} = 1 \div \dfrac{4}{9} = 1 \times \dfrac{9}{4} = \dfrac{9}{4}$

Division by zero

Division is like repeated subtraction. How many times can you take 3 away from 12? You can take 3 away four times. $12 \div 3 = 4$.
How many times can you take zero away from a number? The answer is, as many as you like! It won't change the number.
Therefore dividing by zero gives an answer of infinity.
If you think about it you can see that $8 \div 2 = 4$ because $2 + 2 + 2 + 2 = 8$.
Thinking about $5 \div 0$, you would never get 5, however many zeros you added togther.
So $5 \div 0 = \infty$ (infinity)

Rational numbers are numbers which can be represented as:

- integers (whole numbers)
- fractions
- finite or terminating decimals (i.e. decimals that do not go on for ever)
- recurring decimals.

Irrational numbers

Irrational numbers are numbers which are not rational!

When an irrational number is written as a decimal, it goes on and on indefinitely, without any pattern.

The main types you will see are:

- π
- square roots of non-square numbers, e.g. $\sqrt{2}$, $\sqrt{5}$

The words 'rational' and 'irrational' have the same origins as the word 'ratio'. Any rational number can be written as a ratio (or fraction). Even an integer or whole number can be written as a ratio, for example:
$4 = \dfrac{4}{1}$

Surds

A surd is a number that includes the square root of a positive non-square integer (whole number).

Before you start, you should know that
$\sqrt{x} \times \sqrt{x} = (\sqrt{x})^2 = x$

So, for example, $\sqrt{3} \times \sqrt{3} = \sqrt{9}$ or $(\sqrt{3})^2 = 3$
and $\sqrt{5} \times \sqrt{5} = \sqrt{25}$ or $(\sqrt{5})^2 = 5$
Though $\sqrt{5} \times \sqrt{3} = \sqrt{15}$,
$\sqrt{5} + \sqrt{3}$ does **not** equal $\sqrt{8}$

Rewriting surds

Example 1.1

Rewrite $\sqrt{32}$

Solution

Find the largest square number that is a factor of the number under the square root sign; in this case, 16 is the largest square number that goes into 32.

Rewrite the number under the square root as the product of the square number, 16, and the factor that multiplies it to make 32.

$\sqrt{32} = \sqrt{16 \times 2}$

$\quad = \sqrt{16} \times \sqrt{2}$ Separate into the product of two square roots

$\quad = 4\sqrt{2}$ Take the square root of the square number

Note that $\sqrt{xy} = \sqrt{x}\sqrt{y}$ but $\sqrt{x+y} \neq \sqrt{x} + \sqrt{y}$

Exercise 1.1

Rewrite the following square roots:

1	$\sqrt{12}$	**2**	$\sqrt{27}$	**3**	$\sqrt{200}$	**4**	$\sqrt{75}$
5	$\sqrt{28}$	**6**	$\sqrt{24}$	**7**	$\sqrt{50}$	**8**	$\sqrt{48}$
9	$\sqrt{72}$	**10**	$\sqrt{20}$				

Answers 1.1

1 $2\sqrt{3}$	**2** $3\sqrt{3}$	**3** $10\sqrt{2}$	**4** $5\sqrt{3}$		**5** $2\sqrt{7}$	**6** $2\sqrt{6}$	**7** $5\sqrt{2}$	**8** $4\sqrt{3}$	**9** $6\sqrt{2}$ **10** $2\sqrt{5}$

Adding and subtracting surds

To add or subtract surds, rewrite them and you should find that the part of each number with the square root is the same.

Example 1.2

Simplify $\sqrt{300} - \sqrt{12}$

Solution

$\sqrt{300} - \sqrt{12} = \sqrt{100} \times \sqrt{3} - \sqrt{4} \times \sqrt{3}$

$\quad\quad = 10\sqrt{3} - 2\sqrt{3}$

$\quad\quad = 8\sqrt{3}$

Example 1.3

Simplify $\sqrt{63} + \sqrt{28}$

Solution

$\sqrt{63} + \sqrt{28} = \sqrt{9} \times \sqrt{7} + \sqrt{4} \times \sqrt{7}$

$\quad\quad = 3\sqrt{7} + 2\sqrt{7}$

$\quad\quad = 5\sqrt{7}$

Exercise 1.2

Simplify these expressions.

1	$\sqrt{50} + \sqrt{98}$	**2**	$\sqrt{45} + \sqrt{20}$
3	$\sqrt{160} + \sqrt{90}$	**4**	$\sqrt{200} + \sqrt{32}$
5	$\sqrt{600} + \sqrt{54}$	**6**	$\sqrt{500} - \sqrt{125} + \sqrt{20}$
7	$\sqrt{108} - \sqrt{27}$	**8**	$\sqrt{63} - \sqrt{7}$

Answers 1.2

1 $\sqrt{25} \times \sqrt{2} + \sqrt{49} \times \sqrt{2} = 5\sqrt{2} + 7\sqrt{2} = 12\sqrt{2}$

2 $\sqrt{9} \times \sqrt{5} + \sqrt{4} \times \sqrt{5} = 3\sqrt{5} + 2\sqrt{5} = 5\sqrt{5}$

3 $\sqrt{16} \times \sqrt{10} + \sqrt{9} \times \sqrt{10} = 4\sqrt{10} + 3\sqrt{10} = 7\sqrt{10}$

4 $\sqrt{100} \times \sqrt{2} + \sqrt{16} \times \sqrt{2} = 10\sqrt{2} + 4\sqrt{2} = 14\sqrt{2}$

5 $\sqrt{100} \times \sqrt{6} + \sqrt{9} \times \sqrt{6} = 10\sqrt{6} + 3\sqrt{6} = 13\sqrt{6}$

6 $\sqrt{100} \times \sqrt{5} - \sqrt{25} \times \sqrt{5} + \sqrt{4} \times \sqrt{5}$
$= 10\sqrt{5} - 5\sqrt{5} + 2\sqrt{5} = 7\sqrt{5}$

7 $\sqrt{36} \times \sqrt{3} - \sqrt{9} \times \sqrt{3} = 6\sqrt{3} - 3\sqrt{3} = 3\sqrt{3}$

8 $\sqrt{9} \times \sqrt{7} - \sqrt{7} = 3\sqrt{7} - \sqrt{7} = 2\sqrt{7}$

Rationalising the denominator

In this context, this means writing the denominator as a whole number, not a surd. To rationalise the denominator of a fraction, multiply the top and bottom of the fraction by the surd that appears in the denominator.

Example 1.4

Write the fraction below with a rational denominator.

$$\frac{2}{\sqrt{3}}$$

Solution

Multiply the top and bottom of the fraction by the surd on the denominator, i.e. $\sqrt{3}$

$$\frac{2}{\sqrt{3}} = \frac{2}{\sqrt{3}} \times \frac{\sqrt{3}}{\sqrt{3}} = \frac{2\sqrt{3}}{3}$$

The denominator has changed from $\sqrt{3}$, an irrational number, to 3, a rational number.

Exercise 1.3

Rationalise the denominators in the following:

a) $\dfrac{4}{\sqrt{2}}$ b) $\dfrac{18}{\sqrt{3}}$ c) $\dfrac{6}{\sqrt{5}}$ d) $\dfrac{3}{\sqrt{7}}$

Answers 1.3

a) $2\sqrt{2}$ b) $6\sqrt{3}$ c) $\dfrac{6\sqrt{5}}{5}$ d) $\dfrac{3\sqrt{7}}{7}$

Expanding expressions with surds

If the expression includes brackets, you need to multiply them out carefully.

For double brackets, turn to FOIL in Chapter 3 (page 28).

Example 1.5

Expand $\sqrt{3}(\sqrt{3} + 2)$

Solution

$\sqrt{3}(\sqrt{3} + 2) = \sqrt{3} \times \sqrt{3} + 2\sqrt{3} = 3 + 2\sqrt{3}$

Remember that $\sqrt{3} \times \sqrt{3} = \sqrt{9} = 3$

Example 1.6

Expand $(\sqrt{5} + 4)(\sqrt{5} - 2)$, giving your answer in the form $p\sqrt{q} + r$, where p, q and r are integers (whole numbers).

Solution

Using FOIL:

$(\sqrt{5} + 4)(\sqrt{5} - 2) = \sqrt{5} \times \sqrt{5} - 2\sqrt{5} + 4\sqrt{5} - 8$
$\qquad\qquad\qquad\qquad = 5 + 2\sqrt{5} - 8 = 2\sqrt{5} - 3$

Exercise 1.4

Expand the following, simplifying your answers as much as possible:

1 $\sqrt{7}(2\sqrt{7} - 1)$ 2 $\sqrt{2}(3\sqrt{2} + 5)$

3 $(2\sqrt{3} - 1)(\sqrt{3} + 2)$ 4 $(\sqrt{2} + 5)(3\sqrt{2} - 4)$

Answers 1.4

1 $14 - \sqrt{7}$ 2 $6 + 5\sqrt{2}$

3 $4 + 3\sqrt{3}$ 4 $11\sqrt{2} - 14$

Formulae

Triplets help you to remember formulae, which are used in many questions throughout this book.

To find a letter, first cover it up or cross it out. If the remaining letters are:

- on the same level, multiply them, or
- on different levels, divide the top by the bottom.

Distance, Speed, Time

$D = S \times T \qquad S = \dfrac{D}{T} \qquad T = \dfrac{D}{S}$

Remember **D**owning **St**.

You may have used S for distance and V or v for velocity in place of speed. If so, you need **S**atellite **TV**, in the form:

$S = T \times V \qquad T = \dfrac{S}{V} \qquad V = \dfrac{S}{T}$

Amount, Rate, Time

Remember **ART**.

$A = R \times T \qquad R = \dfrac{A}{T} \qquad T = \dfrac{A}{R}$

Density formula

This is **M**aths for the **V**ery **D**ense!

$M = V \times D \qquad V = \dfrac{M}{D} \qquad D = \dfrac{M}{V}$

mass = volume × density
$(M = V \times D)$ etc.

Example 1.7

A bus travels at 45 km/h. How far does it travel in 3 hours and 25 minutes?

You may see speeds such as 45 km/h expressed in other ways, such as 45 km per hour, or 45 km h⁻¹. They all mean the same thing.

Solution

Firstly, do not write 3 hours 25 minutes as 3.25. Instead, work it out like this.

3 hours 25 minutes = $3\frac{25}{60}$ or 3 [a b/c] 25 [a b/c] 60

You are asked for the distance. Cover or cross out D. S and T are on the same level, so you multiply them.

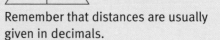

$D = S \times T$
$= 45 \times 3 \lrcorner 25 \lrcorner 60$
$= 153.75$ km

Remember that distances are usually given in decimals.

4

Example 1.8

Beer is poured from a barrel at a rate of 25 ml per second. How long does it take to fill a 1 litre jug? (1 litre = 1000 ml)

Solution

$$T = \frac{A}{R} = \frac{1000}{25} = 40 \text{ seconds}$$

Don't mix units.
Convert litres into ml before you start a question like this.

Example 1.9

A cyclist travels 36 kilometres in 1 hour and 30 minutes. Find his average speed in kilometres per hour.

Solution

$$S = \frac{D}{T} = \frac{36}{1.5} = 24 \text{ km/h}$$

Did you get the right answer? If you didn't it's probably because you wrote the time as 1.30 instead of 1 hour 30 minutes = 1.5 hours.

Exercise 1.5

1 An old coach horse could travel 120 kilometres in 5 hours and 15 minutes. What was its average speed?
2 A group of men can unload grain at the rate of 6 cubic metres per hour. How long does it take them to unload 44 cubic metres? Give your answer in hours and minutes.
3 Duck feathers weighing 0.81 kg are packed into a box of volume 54 000 cubic centimetres. Find the density of the feathers, in g/cm³.

Answers 1.5

3 0.015 g/cm³
2 7.33 hours = 7 hours 20 minutes
1 22.9 km/h

TAKE A BREAK

When you come back, it'll be about time for some approximations.

Approximation

Rounding

Remember, *when you round:*

if the last digit is 0, 1, 2, 3 or 4 you ignore it,

if the last digit is 5, 6, 7, 8 or 9 you round up.

When you are using decimal places or significant figures, the above rules apply, but always read the question carefully. If, for instance, your answer suggests that 5.2 coaches are required to carry a certain number of people, you will need to round up to 6 to avoid stranded passengers!

If your final answer requires, say, two decimal places, either use your calculator's memory or else round to four decimal places until you need the final answer, to avoid inaccuracies.

Approximation to the nearest unit

Rounding errors

Example 1.10

If a number, rounded to one decimal place, becomes 3.4, what is the possible range of the original number?

Strictly, the original number could be anywhere between 3.35, the lower bound, and 3.44999 …, the upper bound. However, when dealing with this type of question, we take the upper bound as 3.45.

Solution

Method 1

To find the upper bound, you simply put a 5 at the end of the decimal.

To find the lower bound, you subtract 1 from the last digit and put a 5 at the end.

Taking 1 from 3.4 gives 3.3, which then becomes 3.35 by putting a 5 at the end.

Upper bound = 3.45

Lower bound = 3.35

Method 2

Write the number you are given.

Put zero beneath each digit after the decimal point, then put a 5 at the end. This creates a new number which you must subtract to get the lower bound and add to get the upper bound.

i.e. 3.4

    0.05

Taking away: 3.4 − 0.05 gives 3.35, the lower bound.

Adding: 3.4 + 0.05 gives 3.45, the upper bound.

Method 3

Draw a number line as shown.

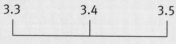

Then insert the midpoints:

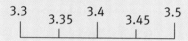

Interval approximation

An interval approximation is simply a way of writing the lower and upper bounds. Your answer will contain one more digit than the number in the question. Interval approximation is the opposite of rounding.

Example 1.11

Write, as an interval approximation, 6.13 correct to 2 d.p.

Solution

A question like this requires an answer containing three decimal places, although at first glance it seems to ask for two.

6.12   6.13   6.14
   6.125   6.135

−0.005   +0.005

Lower bound: 6.13 − 0.005 = 6.125

Upper bound: 6.13 + 0.005 = 6.135

Calculating rounding errors

Remember that the larger the number you divide by, the smaller the answer, and vice versa.

Example 1.12

The area of a rectangular field is 42 200 m², and its length is 278 m, both correct to three significant figures. Find the greatest and smallest possible breadths of the field, correct to one decimal place.

Solution

The interval approximation of the length is 277.5 to 278.5.

The interval approximation for the area is 42 150 to 42 250.

The largest breadth is

$$\frac{\text{largest area}}{\text{smallest length}} = \frac{42\,250}{277.5} = 152.3\,\text{m}$$

The smallest possible breadth is

$$\frac{\text{smallest area}}{\text{largest length}} = \frac{42\,150}{278.5} = 151.3\,\text{m}$$

Exercise 1.6

1   Ten cameras in a box each weigh 1.2 kg to the nearest 0.1 kg. Find the lower and upper bounds for the weight of the ten cameras.

2   A pencil is found to measure 18 cm to the nearest cm. What is the longest possible length of the pencil?

3   The area of a rectangle is given as 14.1 cm² to the nearest 0.1 cm² and its width is given as 6.2 cm to the nearest 0.1 cm. Calculate the upper and lower bounds of its length.

4   Write 3.24 as an interval approximation correct to 2 d.p.

Answers 1.6

1   11.5 and 12.5 kg   2   18.5 cm
3   2.30 cm and 2.25 cm   4   3.235, 3.245

 TAKE A BREAK

The indications are that you're about ready for another break!

Indices

In the number 2^3, the 3 is called the **power** or the **index**. The plural of index is indices. The 2 is called the base number.

2^3 means 3 lots of 2 multiplied together or $2 \times 2 \times 2$ **not** 2×3

$2^{\frac{1}{2}}$ means $\sqrt{2}$ and $2^{\frac{1}{3}}$ means $\sqrt[3]{2}$

Rules

1. *You can only simplify indices when the base numbers are the same.*
2. *When dividing or multiplying powers of the same number remember TIP and DIM.*

   *For multiplication use **TIP***
   ***T**imes $\Rightarrow$ **I**ndices **P**lus* $x^2 \times x^5 = x^7$

   *For division use **DIM***
   ***D**ivide $\Rightarrow$ **I**ndices **M**inus* $\dfrac{x^9}{x^4} = x^5$

   *For powers of variables with indices, use **PIT***
   ***P**ower $\Rightarrow$ **I**ndices **T**imes* $(x^2)^3 = x^6$

   $$\sqrt[3]{(x^7)} = (x^7)^{\frac{1}{3}} = x^{\frac{7}{3}}$$

Example 1.13

Simplify these by expressing them as powers of 3.

a) $3^2 \times 3^5$ b) $3^7 \div 3^2$ c) $3^2 + 3^5$
d) $3^5 \times 2^3$ e) $3^3 \div 3^2$

Solution

a) $3^2 \times 3^5 = 3^7$

b) $3^7 \div 3^2 = 3^5$

c) $3^2 + 3^5$ Cannot be simplified as a power of 3.

d) $3^5 \times 2^3$ Cannot be simplified because the base numbers are different.

e) $3^3 \div 3^2 = 3$

Negative and fractional indices

A negative power means '1 over' (or a reciprocal).

Negative indices

$x^{-1} = \dfrac{1}{x}$ $x^{-2} = \dfrac{1}{x^2}$ $2x^{-3} = \dfrac{2}{x^3}$

Fractional indices

$x^{\frac{1}{2}} = \sqrt{x}$ $x^{\frac{1}{3}} = \sqrt[3]{x}$ $x^{\frac{2}{3}} = \sqrt[3]{x^2}$

Indices of zero

Any number to the power of zero equals 1:
e.g. $10^0 = 1$ $x^0 = 1$

Example 1.14

Evaluate $\left(\dfrac{25}{16}\right)^{\frac{3}{2}}$

Evaluate just means 'find the value of'.

Solution

Start by splitting the power into a multiple of $\frac{1}{2}$ and 3. Use brackets and put the half first:

$$\left(\frac{25}{16}\right)^{\frac{3}{2}} = \left(\left(\frac{25}{16}\right)^{\frac{1}{2}}\right)^3$$

Then evaluate $\left(\dfrac{25}{16}\right)^{\frac{1}{2}}$, which is the same as

$$\sqrt{\left(\frac{25}{16}\right)} = \frac{5}{4}$$

Then $\left(\dfrac{25}{16}\right)^{\frac{3}{2}} = \left(\left(\dfrac{25}{16}\right)^{\frac{1}{2}}\right)^3 = \left(\dfrac{5}{4}\right)^3 = \dfrac{125}{64}$

Working out the root part first makes the denominator and numerator smaller, so it is much easier to work with.

Example 1.15

Evaluate $\left(\dfrac{27}{8}\right)^{-\frac{2}{3}}$

Solution

Split the power into a multiple of $\frac{1}{3}$, 2 and -1:

$$\left(\frac{27}{8}\right)^{-\frac{2}{3}} = \left(\left(\left(\frac{27}{8}\right)^{\frac{1}{3}}\right)^2\right)^{-1} = \left(\left(\frac{3}{2}\right)^2\right)^{-1} = \left(\frac{9}{4}\right)^{-1} = \frac{4}{9}$$

Exercise 1.7

Write the following powers as integers or improper fractions (where appropriate):

1 5^{-1} 2 $\left(\dfrac{3}{2}\right)^{-1}$ 3 $8^{\frac{2}{3}}$ 4 $9^{\frac{3}{2}}$

5 $\left(\dfrac{4}{9}\right)^{\frac{1}{2}}$ 6 $\left(\dfrac{64}{27}\right)^{\frac{1}{3}}$ 7 $\left(\dfrac{1}{125}\right)^{-\frac{1}{3}}$ 8 $\left(\dfrac{1}{36}\right)^{-\frac{1}{2}}$

9 $\left(\dfrac{4}{9}\right)^{-\frac{3}{2}}$ 10 $\left(\dfrac{64}{125}\right)^{-\frac{2}{3}}$

Answers 1.7

9 $\dfrac{27}{8}$ 10 $\dfrac{25}{16}$

5 $\dfrac{2}{3}$ 6 $\dfrac{4}{3}$ 7 5   8 6

1 $\dfrac{1}{5}$ 2 $\dfrac{2}{3}$ 3 4   4 27

Example 1.16

Write $\dfrac{\sqrt{x}}{yz^3}$ in the form $x^p y^q z^r$

Solution

$x^{\frac{1}{2}} y^{-1} z^{-3}$

Example 1.17

Simplify: **i)** $x^{-2} x^3 \sqrt{x}$ **ii)** $\sqrt{x^2 y^6}$

Solution

i) Using TIP, $x^{-2} x^3 \sqrt{x} = x^{-2+3+0.5} = x^{1.5}$ or $x^{\frac{3}{2}}$

ii) Using PIT, $\sqrt{x^2 y^6} = (x^2 y^6)^{0.5} = xy^3$

Note that this does not work for the power of a sum:

$\sqrt{x^2 + y^2}$ is not $x + y$, and $(x + y)^2$ is not $x^2 + y^2$

Example 1.18

Evaluate $9^3 \div 9^5$.

Express your answer:

a) as a power of 9

b) as a fraction.

Solution

a) $9^3 \div 9^5 = 9^{-2}$

b) $9^{-2} = \dfrac{1}{9^2} = \dfrac{1}{81}$

Exercise 1.8

1 Simplify $7^2 \times 7^5$, giving your answer as a power of 7.

2 Simplify $3^2 \div 3^5$, giving your answer:
   a) as a power of 3   **b)** as a fraction.

3 Write $4^{-\frac{1}{2}}$ as a fraction.

4 Simplify $(x \times x^5) \div \sqrt{x}$

5 Write $\dfrac{\sqrt{x}}{yz^2}$ in the form $x^a y^b z^c$

Answers 1.8

5 $a = \frac{1}{2}$, $b = -1$, $c = -2$

4 $x^{5\frac{1}{2}}$ or $x^{\frac{11}{2}}$ 3 $\frac{1}{2}$

2 a) 3^{-3} b) $\frac{1}{27}$ 1 7^7

Unknown indices

Example 1.19

Find x where

a) $4^x = 8$

b) $9^{x+1} = 27^x$

c) $25^{x-2} = \dfrac{1}{\sqrt{5}}$

Solution

a) Both 4 and 8 are powers of 2, so rewrite them as such:
$(2^2)^x = 2^3$
$2^{2x} = 2^3$

Then equate the powers and solve:
$2x = 3$
$x = 1.5$

b) As both 9 and 27 are powers of 3, rewrite them as such:
$(3^2)^{x+1} = (3^3)^x$

Expand the brackets (remembering to multiply the 1 as well as the x by 2):
$3^{2x+2} = 3^{3x}$

Equate the powers and solve:
$2x + 2 = 3x$
$x = 2$

c) Write both 25 and $\dfrac{1}{\sqrt{5}}$ as powers of 5:
$(5^2)^{x-2} = 5^{-\frac{1}{2}}$

Expand the brackets, remembering that $2(x - 2) = 2x - 4$:
$5^{2x-4} = 5^{-\frac{1}{2}}$

Equate the indices and solve:
$2x - 4 = -\frac{1}{2}$
$x = 1.75$ or $1\frac{3}{4}$

Exercise 1.9

1 Solve the following equations to find x:
   a) $16^x = 8$
   b) $8^{x-3} = 4^{2x}$
   c) $9^{x+1} = \dfrac{1}{\sqrt{27}}$

2 **a)** If $\sqrt[3]{4} = 2^p$, find p.
   b) The base of a triangle is $\dfrac{1}{\sqrt{2}}$ and its height is $\sqrt[3]{4}$. If its area is 2^q, find q.

Answers 1.9

1 a) $(2^4)^x = 2^3$

$4x = 3$

$x = \frac{3}{4}$

b) $(2^3)^{x-3} = (2^2)^{2x}$

$3x - 6 = 4x$

$x = -9$

c) $(3^2)^{x+1} = 3^{-1.5}$

$2x + 2 = -1.5$

$2x = -3.5$

$x = -1.75$

2 a) $\sqrt[3]{4} = (2^2)^{\frac{1}{3}} = 2^{\frac{2}{3}}$, so $p = \frac{2}{3}$

b) Area of triangle $= \frac{1}{2}bh$

$= \frac{1}{2} \times \frac{1}{\sqrt{2}} \times \sqrt[3]{4}$

$= 2^{-1} \times 2^{-\frac{1}{2}} \times 2^{\frac{2}{3}}$

$= 2^{-\frac{5}{6}}$

so $q = -\frac{5}{6}$

Standard form or standard index form

This is a short method of writing very large or very small numbers.

Numbers in standard form are written as $p \times 10^q$ where $1 \le p < 10$ and q is an integer.

Example 1.20

The speed of light is approximately 300 000 000 m/s.

a) Write 300 000 000 in standard form.

b) How far does light travel in 1 year? Give your answers in metres in standard index form.

c) How long does it take light to travel 1 metre? Give your answer in seconds in standard index form.

Solution

a) 3×10^8

b) Number of seconds in a year

$= 60 \times 60 \times 24 \times 365$

$= 31\,536\,000$

In a year, light travels

$3 \times 10^8 \times 31\,536\,000 = 9.46 \times 10^{15}$ metres

c) Time $= \dfrac{\text{Distance}}{\text{Speed}}$

$= \dfrac{1}{3 \times 10^8} = 3.3 \times 10^{-9}$ seconds

When you have converted a large or small number to standard form, check on your calculator if you are in any doubt. For example:

3.42×10^4 [3] [.] [4] [2] [EXP] [4] [=]

6.7×10^{-5} [6] [.] [7] [EXP] [(-)] [5] [=]

On some calculators, you will find [EE] instead of [EXP]. You may find [+/-] instead of [(-)].

If your calculator does not change the standard form number into its equivalent, try doing it the other way round: e.g. enter 0.000067 and press [=].

If you can say, 'times 10 to the', replace it with [EXP] or [EE].

Do not press [×] [1] [0] [EXP]

Example 1.21

What is the product of 3.5×10^{120} and 7.2×10^{108}? Give your answer in standard index form.

Solution

These numbers are too large for most calculators.

$(3.5 \times 10^{120}) \times (7.2 \times 10^{108}) = 25.2 \times 10^{228}$ using TIP.

Converting to standard index form:

$25.2 \times 10^{228} = 2.52 \times 10 \times 10^{228}$

$= 2.52 \times 10^{229}$

Exercise 1.10

1 Find k if $\sqrt{8} = 4^k$

2 Evaluate $(1.2 \times 10^{200}) \div (4.0 \times 10^{145})$ Write your answer in standard index form.

Answers 1.10

1 Express both sides as powers of 2

$\sqrt{8} = 4^k$

$(2^3)^{0.5} = (2^2)^k$

$2^{1.5} = 2^{2k}$

Equate powers

$1.5 = 2k$

$k = 0.75$

2 $\dfrac{1.2 \times 10^{200}}{4.0 \times 10^{145}} = 0.3 \times 10^{55}$

because $1.2 \div 4 = 0.3$ and using DIM, $200 - 145 = 55$

$= 0.3 \times 10 \times 10^{54}$

$= 3 \times 10^{54}$

Multiplying numbers written in standard form

Remember that when you are multiplying four numbers, you can multiply them in any order. This means that when you multiply two numbers in standard form you can multiply the first parts of the numbers, then the second parts of the numbers. Then you must make sure your final answer is in standard form.

Example 1.22

Evaluate $(3.1 \times 10^9) \times (4.0 \times 10^7)$ without using a calculator. Write your answer in standard form.

Solution

Remove the brackets and write the first parts of the two numbers next to each other, then the second parts of the numbers:
$3.1 \times 4.0 \times 10^9 \times 10^7 = 12.4 \times 10^{16}$

This must now be written in standard form.
$1.24 \times 10 \times 10^{16} = 1.24 \times 10^{17}$

Dividing numbers written in standard form

Divide the first parts of the numbers, then the second parts of the numbers, then make sure your final answer is in standard form.

Example 1.23

Evaluate $\dfrac{6.2 \times 10^8}{2.0 \times 10^3}$

Write your answer in standard form.

Solution

$(6.2 \times 10^8) \div (2.0 \times 10^3) = (6.2 \div 2.0) \times (10^8 \div 10^3)$
$= 3.1 \times 10^5$

Exercise 1.11

Evaluate the following, giving your answers in standard form. Try to do them without using a calculator. Then use a calculator to check your answers.

1 $(4.2 \times 10^3) \times (1.5 \times 10^4)$

2 $(7.4 \times 10^{-3}) \times (6.5 \times 10^{-5})$

3 $\dfrac{3.6 \times 10^{11}}{1.2 \times 10^5}$

4 $\dfrac{7.2 \times 10^{-5}}{2.4 \times 10^4}$

Adding and subtracting numbers written in standard form

There are two methods of adding and subtracting numbers written in standard form without using a calculator.

You can convert the numbers back into regular form, add or subtract them, then convert them back into standard form.

Example 1.24

Evaluate $2.2 \times 10^7 + 1.6 \times 10^6$. Write your answer in standard form.

Solution

$2.2 \times 10^7 + 1.6 \times 10^6 = 22\,000\,000$
$ 1\,600\,000 +$
$= 23\,600\,000$
$= 2.36 \times 10^7$

Alternatively, you can write the two numbers with the same power of 10, then add or subtract the two numbers. Make sure you have written your final answer in the required form.

Example 1.25

Evaluate $2.2 \times 10^7 + 1.6 \times 10^6$. Write your answer in standard form.

Solution

Write the first number using 10^6:
$2.2 \times 10 \times 10^6 = 22 \times 10^6$
Then add:
$22 \times 10^6 + 1.6 \times 10^6 = 23.6 \times 10^6$
Write the answer in standard form:
$= 2.36 \times 10 \times 10^6 = 2.36 \times 10^7$
Or you could have written the second number using 10^7:
$2.2 \times 10^7 + 1.6 \times 10^{-1} \times 10^7 = 2.2 \times 10^7 + 0.16 \times 10^7$
$= 2.36 \times 10^7$

Exercise 1.12

Evaluate the following without using a calculator, giving your answers in standard form:

1 $5.4 \times 10^6 + 2.3 \times 10^5$

2 $3.8 \times 10^8 + 8.6 \times 10^7$

3 $6.7 \times 10^{10} - 8.6 \times 10^9$

4 $1.8 \times 10^{-3} - 7.9 \times 10^{-4}$

5 $1.6 \times 10^{-8} - 9.3 \times 10^{-9}$

Answers 1.12

1 5.63×10^6

2 4.66×10^8

3 5.84×10^{10}

4 1.01×10^{-3}

5 6.7×10^{-9}

 TAKE A BREAK

This is another good place to take a break, before starting the dash for the end of the chapter.

Using your calculator

Examiners often set questions like:

Solve $\dfrac{\sqrt{31.92}}{51.7 - 73^2}$

 Hints & Tips

It is important to remember that your calculator will square or take the square root, then multiply or divide, then add or subtract. By using brackets and sometimes = *you can change this order.*

Example 1.26

Evaluate $\dfrac{18 + 2}{5}$

Solution

You can see that the answer is $20 \div 5 = 4$, but if you keyed in $18 + 2 \div 5$ your calculator would show 18.4 because it would calculate $2 \div 5$ before adding the 18.

You can avoid this by keying in:

| 1 | 8 | + | 2 | = | ÷ | 5 | = |

or

| (| 1 | 8 | + | 2 |) | ÷ | 5 | = |

to give the answer, 4.

Either way, the 18 and the 2 are added before you divide.

Example 1.27

Evaluate $\dfrac{60 + \sqrt{5}}{7.2 - 3.1}$

Solution

$\dfrac{60 + \sqrt{5}}{7.2 - 3.1} = (60 + \sqrt{5}) \div (7.2 - 3.1) = 15.2$ (1 d.p.)

Exercise 1.13

1 Evaluate $\dfrac{\sqrt{5} + 12}{3.4^2 - 6.1}$

2 Evaluate $\dfrac{1}{\sqrt{3} + \sqrt{5}}$

3 Evaluate $f = \dfrac{xy}{\sqrt{x - y}}$ where $x = 3.7$ and $y = -0.2$

4 Find an approximate answer to $\dfrac{3.8 \times 7.9}{0.18 + 1.8}$ showing all your working.

Answers 1.13

1 2.61

2 0.25

3 -0.37

4 $(4 \times 8) \div (0.2 + 1.8) = 32 \div 2 = 16$

 Make sure you know the difference between the x^y (or it may be y^x) and EXP or EE buttons on your calculator.

Converting decimals to fractions

Finite or terminating decimals may be converted as follows.

$0.3 = \dfrac{3}{10}$ $0.14 = \dfrac{14}{100}$ $0.986 = \dfrac{986}{1000}$

Recurring or non-terminating decimals

Multiply your original decimal by a power of 10, depending on the pattern of repeats in the decimal.

Where one digit is repeated in the decimal, multiply by 10 (or 10^1).

For example, 0.55555555 ... or 0.2222222 ...

Where two digits are repeated, multiply by 100 (or 10^2).

For example 0.43434343 ... or 0.76767676 ...

Where three digits are repeated, multiply by 1000 (or 10^3).

For example 0.231231231231 ... or 0.953953953953 ...

The 999 method (a quicker way)

If you have a single digit which is repeated, such as 0.33333 ..., this can be expressed as a digit over 9.

For example $0.33333 \ldots = \frac{3}{9} = \frac{1}{3}$ or $0.88888 \ldots = \frac{8}{9}$

If two numbers are repeated in the decimal, then the decimal can be expressed as the same two numbers over 99.

For example $0.87878787 \ldots = \frac{87}{99} = \frac{29}{33}$ or $0.63636363 \ldots = \frac{63}{99} = \frac{7}{11}$

Similarly for a repeating group of three digits.

For example $0.145145145 \ldots = \frac{145}{999}$ or $0.123123123 \ldots = \frac{123}{999} = \frac{41}{333}$

If you have a recurring decimal that starts with a few different digits followed by repeating numbers, such as 0.123333 ..., you will need to modify this method.

$$0.12333333 \ldots = 0.3333333 \ldots - 0.21$$
$$= \frac{3}{9} - \frac{21}{100}$$
$$= \frac{37}{300} \text{ (\textbf{Check}, using your calculator.)}$$

Remember to give your answer in its lowest terms.

Example 1.28

Express **a)** 0.47474747 ... and **b)** 0.127777 ... in the form $\frac{a}{b}$ where a and b are integers.

Solution

The aim is to find two numbers with the same recurring decimal after the decimal point.

a) Let $x =$ 0.47474747 ...   (1)
   $100x = 47.474747 \ldots$ (2)
   $99x = 47$ (2) − (1)
   $x = \dfrac{47}{99}$

b) Let $x =$ 0.127777 ...
   $100x =$ 12.7777 ...   (1)
   $1000x = 127.7777 \ldots$ (2)
   $900x = 115$ (2) − (1)
   $x = \dfrac{115}{900} = \dfrac{23}{180}$

Exercise 1.14

1 Write each of these numbers as a fraction.
   a) 0.242424242 ...   **b)** 0.562424242 ...
2 Write 0.345345345 ... as a fraction.
3 If $x = 0.516516516 \ldots$, evaluate:
   a) $1000x$ **b)** $999x$
   c) x as a rational number in the form $\dfrac{a}{b}$

 TAKE A BREAK

Take another break to gather your strength for some hard work!

Exam-type questions 1

1 Write 5300 as an interval approximation correct to 3 sig. figs.
2 Evaluate the following.
   a) $\dfrac{12.76 - 4.71}{4.90 + 1.77}$ **b)** $\dfrac{11.1^2}{\sqrt{9.4 - 2.1}}$
   c) $\dfrac{5.6}{(1.9 - 0.7)^2}$
3 A particle travels 1.75 m in 1.26 seconds.
   a) What is its speed in m/s?
   b) What is its speed in km per hour?
   c) Assuming that the given information has been rounded to 3 sig. figs., find the upper and lower bounds of its speed, in m/s.
4 Use the formula $V = \frac{1}{4}\pi xy\sqrt{x^2 - 2y^2}$ to find V when $x = 1.4$ and $y = 0.6$.
5 The number 2.38 has been written correct to 2 d.p. State its lower and upper bounds.
6 The speed of light is approximately 3×10^8 m/s. Find the time it takes, in minutes, to travel 7.2×10^{10} metres.
7 The mass of an object is 1750 grams, correct to 3 sig. figs. Its volume is 272 cm³ correct to 3 sig. figs. Find the upper and lower bounds of its density, stating the units.
8 Use the formula $C = \dfrac{a + b}{a - b^2}$ to find C when
   $a = -41.7$ and $b = 32.6$. Give your answer correct to 3 sig. figs.
9 Express each of the following in the form $\dfrac{a}{b}$ where a and b are integers.
   a) 0.666 ...   **b)** 0.720720720 ...
   c) 0.2133333333 ...

---

10 If $x = 0.162162162 \ldots$ find:

   a) $1000x$ **b)** $999x$

   c) Express x as a fraction in its lowest terms.

11 Simplify the following where possible.

   a) $27^{-\frac{1}{3}}$ expressing your answer as a fraction

   b) $\dfrac{5^{-2} \times 5^3}{\sqrt{5}}$ giving your answer as a power of 5

   c) $3^2 + 3^4$

   d) $25 \div 5^4$ giving your answer

      i) as a power of 5,   **ii)** as a fraction.

Answers

1 5295, 5305

2 a) 1.21   **b)** 45.6   **c)** 3.9

3 a) 1.39 m/s   **b)** 5 km/h

   c) $1.755 \div 1.255 = 1.40$ m/s,

   $1.745 \div 1.265 = 1.38$ m/s

4 0.73 correct to 2 d.p.   **5** 2.375, 2.385

6 $(7.2 \times 10^{10}) \div (3 \times 10^8) = 240$ seconds

   $= 4$ minutes

7 $1755 \div 271.5 = 6.46 \, \text{g/cm}^3$,

   $1745 \div 272.5 = 6.40 \, \text{g/cm}^3$

8 0.008824

9 a) $\dfrac{2}{3}$ **b)** $\dfrac{111}{80}$ **c)** $\dfrac{16}{75}$

10 a) 162.162162...   **b)** 162   **c)** $\dfrac{6}{37}$

11 a) $\dfrac{1}{3}$ **b)** $5^{\frac{3}{2}}$

   c) 90 (cannot be simplified as a power of 3)

   d) i) 5^{-2} **ii)** $\dfrac{1}{25}$

Proportion

Would you like one quick and easy method guaranteed to solve all these questions?

1 If 74 members of an archery club can shoot 333 arrows in 5 minutes, how many arrows could 52 members shoot in the same time and at the same rate?

2 In 1862 the population of a town increased by 15%, or 252 people. What was the population in 1861?

3 A pie chart represents 300 members of a swimming club. How many degrees represent 80 members?

4 If a garden centre offered 126 flower bulbs for £4.50, how much would 350 bulbs cost?

We'll show you our method using a really easy example so that you can see how it works.

Example 2.1

Five notebooks cost £15. Find the cost of seven notebooks.

Solution

This is probably the method you used in the past.

5 cost £15

1 costs £15 ÷ 5 = £3

7 cost £3 × 7 = £21

X-Direct Method

Step 1 Set out the information in a table.

	Books	Cost (£)
I know	5	15
I need	7	

Make sure you put the numbers under the right heading!

Step 2 Draw in the diagonal X as shown.

Books   Cost (£)

5   15

7

Step 3 Apply X-Direct.

Multiply the two numbers connected by a diagonal line (here 7 and 15) and divide by the other number (here 5).

$$\text{Answer} = \frac{7 \times 15}{5} = 21$$

Once you get the hang of this, it's really quick and easy.

Proportionality questions are easy to spot because they usually include the words 'is proportional to', 'is directly proportional to' or 'varies directly with'.

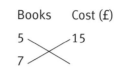

X-Direct appears throughout this book, solving a whole range of different problems.

Answers to Questions 1–4

1   Members   Arrows

74   333

52

$$\frac{52 \times 333}{74} = 234$$

2   Percentage   People

15   252

100

$$\frac{252 \times 100}{15} = 1680$$

3   Degrees   Members

360   300

          80

$$\frac{360 \times 80}{300} = 96°$$

4   Bulbs   Cost (£)

126   4.50

350

$$\frac{350 \times 4.5}{126} = £12.50$$

Exercise 2.1

1. A recipe for 24 blueberry muffins takes 210 grams of butter. How many muffins could you make if you use 280 grams of butter?
2. A barman can make 150 cocktails from 27 litres of cola. How many cocktails could he make with 4.5 litres?
3. If $153.60 is worth 351.50 Mexican pesos, how much is 623.20 Mexican pesos worth?

Answers 2.1

1 32   2 25   3 $272.33

STOP TAKE A BREAK

Take a short break before you tackle percentages.

Percentages

Percentages feature prominently throughout GCSE Maths papers, so this section may help you pick up some valuable marks!

If you have a method which works for you, then continue to use it. If not, try X-Direct.

Percentages using X-Direct

One hundred per cent, or 100%, means the whole, original or total amount.

This, unbelievably, is almost all you have to know to use this method.

Type 1 – finding a percentage of a number

Example 2.2

What is 35% of 210?

Solution

100% is the original amount of 210.

We need to find the number that is 35%.

Number   Percentage (%)

210   100

35

Using X-Direct, $\dfrac{210 \times 35}{100} = 73.5$

So your answer, as it would be in the Number column, is 73.5.

Type 2 – finding one number as a percentage of another

Example 2.3

In a country town, 35 out of 112 people questioned owned horses. Express this as a percentage.

Solution

100% refers to the total number of people, i.e. 112.

People   Percentage (%)

112   100

35

Using X-Direct, $\dfrac{35 \times 100}{112} = 31.25\%$

As this answer would go in the Percentage column, the answer is 31.25% (or 31% to the nearest whole number).

Type 3 – when the figure that you are given does not refer to 100%

Example 2.4

A bank was broken into and 5% of the amount of money stolen was offered as a reward for information. If the reward was £11 200, how much was stolen?

Solution

The original amount was 100%.

Percentage   Pounds (£)

100

5   11 200

Using X-Direct, $\dfrac{100 \times 11\,200}{5} = £224\,000$

Can you see that it does not matter where the gap in the table is, as long as you keep the numbers in the correct columns, and the numbers that relate to each other are in the same row?

Exercise 2.2

1. An investor owns 74% of the shares in a company. If there are 1600 shares, how many does the investor own?
2. A shop bought goods for £350 and sold them for £448. Express the profit as a percentage of the original cost.

3 One day a postman lost 6% of his post. If he lost 114 letters, how many letters was he carrying originally?

4 A clothes shop reduced all shirts priced at £15.50 by £5.50. Express this reduction as a percentage to the nearest 0.1%.

5 A loan shark charged 125% interest per annum on its loans. If it lent £4000, what would be the interest charged in a year?

6 In a bar, 7.5% of the glasses were smashed. If 240 were broken, how many glasses were there originally?

Answers 2.2

1 1184   2 28%   3 1900
4 35.5%   5 £5000   6 3200

VAT questions

At the time of writing this book, VAT is 17.5%. This is a tax put on most items that you buy in the shops. Questions on VAT are common in exams.

Adding on VAT

Example 2.5

The pre-VAT price of a toy is £58.40. Find the VAT-inclusive price.

Solution

Method 1 Work out 17.5% and add it to the original price.

Price (£)   Percentage (%)

58.40   100

                   17.5

$$\frac{58.40 \times 17.5}{100} = 10.22$$

VAT-inclusive price = £58.40 + £10.22
                    = £68.62

Method 2 Use the VAT-inclusive percentage of 117.5%.

Price (£)   Percentage (%)

58.40   100

                   117.5

VAT-inclusive price = $\frac{58.40 \times 117.5}{100}$
                    = £68.62

Removing the VAT from the VAT-inclusive price

As you saw in the example above, the VAT-inclusive price is 100% + 17.5% = 117.5%.

If you want to find the original price, you want 100%, or if you want to find the VAT, you need the 17.5%.

Example 2.6

A can opener is priced at £31.49 including VAT. Find its price before VAT was added.

Solution

Price (£)   Percentage (%)

31.49   117.5

                   100

Pre-VAT price = $\frac{31.49 \times 100}{117.5}$
              = £26.80

Notice that the price is written as £26.80, not £26.8!

Example 2.7

Find the VAT charged if the price including VAT is £16.92.

Solution

Price (£)   Percentage (%)

16.92   117.5

                   17.5

VAT = $\frac{16.92 \times 17.5}{117.5}$ = £2.52

Exercise 2.3

1 A toy is priced at £57.34 including VAT. Find its price excluding VAT.

2 If the VAT on a computer is £218.75, what is its price including VAT?

3 A CD is priced at £16.45 including VAT. In a sale, Chears Ltd offers 17% off this price, while Rock & Soul Records offer it exclusive of VAT. Which company offers the better deal?

Answers 2.3

1 £48.80   2 £1468.75
3 Chears £13.65, Rock and Soul £14.00, so Chears offers the better deal.

Percentages as multipliers

Adding or subtracting a given percentage

To add or subtract, for example, 3% to an amount, you need to find 103% or 97% of the amount.

$$103\% = \frac{103}{100} = 1.03$$

$$97\% = \frac{97}{100} = 0.97$$

So the simplest way of adding or subtracting 3% is to multiply the number by 1.03 or by 0.97 respectively.

Compound percentages

Example 2.8

A number is increased by 10%, then the answer is increased by 20%. What is the total percentage increase?

Solution

Increasing by 10% is the same as multiplying by 1.10, or 1.1, and increasing by 20% is the same as multiplying by 1.20, or 1.2.

$$x \times 1.1 \times 1.2 = 1.32x$$

Multiplying by 1.32 is the same as increasing by 32%.

Example 2.9

A number is reduced by 30% then increased by 15%. What is the total percentage decrease?

Solution

$$x \times 0.7 \times 1.15 = 0.805x$$

As $1 - 0.805 = 0.195$, multiplying by 0.805 is the same as reducing by 19.5%.

Exponential growth and decay

AP^T amount × percentage^{time}

In this formula, for 'percentage', use this method. When adding 5%, write 1.05; when adding 17%, write 1.17. When subtracting 3%, write 0.97; when subtracting 15%, write 0.85.

Example 2.10

A saver invests £650 at 5% for 7 years. Find the total at the end of this period.

Solution

$$AP^T = 650 \times 1.05^7 = £914.62$$

Example 2.11

A small town's population of 18 000 decreases at the rate of 3 per cent per annum (i.e. per year) for 6 years. Find the total population at the end of this period.

Solution

$AP^T = 18\,000 \times 0.97^6 = 14\,993$ to the nearest person

Exercise 2.4

1 The area of farmland in a region grew by 4% per annum for 10 years. If it was 1400 acres initially, find the area of farmland at the end of the period.

2 After the Gold Rush of 1860, the citizens of a southern US city left at the annual rate of 3.5%. What was the population after 20 years if it was 11 400 during the Gold Rush? Give your answer to the nearest 100 people.

Answers 2.4

1 2072 acres   **2** 5600 people

Do not use the **EXP** *or* **EE** *button on your calculator when you are doing exponential questions. Use* x^y *or* y^x *or* **∧** *.*

 TAKE A BREAK

You deserve a break!

Variation

$y \propto x$ means y is proportional to x

$y \propto x^2$ means y is proportional to x^2

$y \propto \dfrac{1}{x}$ means y is inversely proportional to x

$y \propto \dfrac{1}{x^2}$ means y is inversely proportional to x^2

Replace 'proportional to' with '$= k \times$'.

In 'inversely', change the i to a 1 and the n to an o, then the first five letters give '1 over'.

Thus $y \propto x$ becomes $y = kx$

$y \propto \dfrac{1}{x^2}$ becomes $y = k \times \dfrac{1}{x^2}$ or $y = \dfrac{k}{x^2}$

In questions like these you have to find the constant k using values given for x and y. Then the question will give another value for x or y and you will have to find the missing variable using the value of k that you have calculated.

Example 2.12

y is proportional to x^3. When $x = 1.6$, $y = 17.2$. Find:

a) y when $x = 0.6$

b) x when $y = 196$

Solution

$y \propto x^3$

First find the value of k using the given x and y values.

$$y = kx^3$$

$$17.2 = k(1.6)^3$$

$$17.2 = 4.096k$$

$$k = \frac{17.2}{4.096}$$

$$= 4.2 \text{ correct to 1 d.p.}$$

a) When $x = 0.6$ $\quad y = 4.2x^3$

$$= 4.2 \times 0.6^3$$

$$= 0.91 \text{ correct to 2 d.p.}$$

b) When $y = 196$ $\quad y = 4.2x^3$

$$196 = 4.2x^3$$

$$\frac{196}{4.2} = x^3$$

$$x = \sqrt[3]{\frac{196}{4.2}}$$

$$= 3.6 \text{ correct to 1 d.p.}$$

Remember that the inverse, or opposite, of cubing is cube rooting or working to the power of $\frac{1}{3}$.

Hints & Tips

Example 2.13

y is inversely proportional to x^2 and $x = 0.162$ when $y = 471$. Find:

a) y when $x = 1.34$

b) x when $y = 302$

giving all answers correct to three significant figures.

Solution

Firstly, find k.

$$y \propto \frac{1}{x^2}$$

So $y = \dfrac{k}{x^2}$

$$471 = \frac{k}{(0.162)^2}$$

$$k = 471 \times (0.162)^2$$

$$= 12.36 \text{ to 4 s.f.}$$

To minimise later rounding errors, either use the calculator memory for k or round it initially to four or five significant figures.

a) When $x = 1.34$

$$y = \frac{k}{x^2}$$

$$y = \frac{12.36}{1.34^2}$$

$$= 6.88 \text{ correct to 3 s.f.}$$

b) When $y = 302$

$$302 = \frac{12.36}{x^2}$$

$$302x^2 = 12.36$$

$$x^2 = \frac{12.36}{302} = 0.040\,93$$

$$x = 0.202 \text{ correct to 3 s.f.}$$

Exercise 2.5

1 y is proportional to x^2. If $y = 21.3$ when $x = 7.2$, find:
 a) the value of y when $x = 1.7$
 b) the value of x when $y = 41.3$

2 y is inversely proportional to x^3. If $y = 141.1$ when $x = 1.45$, find:
 a) y when $x = 2.74$
 b) x when $y = 444.3$

3 y varies directly as the cube root of x. If $y = 3.44$ when $x = 71.2$, find:
 a) y when $x = 106.8$
 b) x when $y = 4.75$

4 y varies inversely with the square root of x. If $y = 32.1$ when $x = 43.2$, find:
 a) y when $x = 55.7$
 b) x when $y = 20.1$

Answers 2.5

1 $k = 0.41$ a) $y = 1.2$ b) $x = 10.0$
2 $k = 430.2$ a) $y = 20.9$ b) $x = 0.99$
3 $k = 0.83$ a) $y = 3.94$ b) $x = 187$
4 $k = 211$ a) $y = 28.3$ b) $x = 110.2$

Ratios

Ratios can be calculated by using X-Direct.

Hints & Tips

Example 2.14

Write $5 : 4$ in the ratio:

a) $1 : k$ b) $k : 1$.

Solution

a) 5 ⤫ 4
   1

$$k = \frac{1 \times 4}{5} = 0.8 \quad \text{so } 5 : 4 = 1 : 0.8$$

b) 5 ⤫ 4
   1

$$k = \frac{5 \times 1}{4} = 1.25 \quad \text{so } 5 : 4 = 1.25 : 1$$

Exercise 2.6

1 Pete shares his blueberry muffins with Sam in the ratio $7 : 2$. If his bag contains 36 muffins, how many muffins does each receive? What fraction of the original does Sam receive?

2 Write the ratio $12 : 5$ in the form
   a) $n : 1$ b) $1 : n$.

Answers 2.6

1 Pete gets 28, Sam gets 8; $\frac{2}{9}$

2 a) $2.4 : 1$ b) $1 : 0.42$ or $1 : \frac{5}{12}$

TAKE A BREAK

Before you tackle the exam-type questions take a break.

Exam-type questions 2

1 An art dealer buys a painting for £11 200 and sells it for £13 550. Find his percentage profit based on the original price.

2 A farmer traded 362 cows for 2820 chickens.
   a) How many chickens can you get for 1584 cows?
   b) How many cows can be exchanged for 50 605 chickens?

3 A car goes 18.6 km on 4.4 litres of fuel.
   a) How far does it go on 20 litres?
   b) How many litres would it use to go 100 km?
   Write both answers correct to 3 sig. figs.

4 The VAT added to the price of an article is £5.67. What was the pre-VAT price of the article?

5 The diagram shows the composition of the membership of a Sports Club.

	Under 25	Over 25
Men	36	54
Women	24	36

Calculate, in its simplest form, the ratio of:
   a) males to females
   b) under 25s to over 25s.

6 Express the ratio $5 : 2$ in the form:
   a) $n : 1$
   b) $1 : n$

7 A car is bought for £9250 and sold the following year for £7800. Express the depreciation in value as a percentage of the cost price to the nearest 1%.

8 A prize of £450 is divided among Ranjit, Tom and Nadia in the ratio $6 : 7 : 2$. How much does each receive?

9 y varies directly as x^2 and $y = 72.4$ when $x = 5.1$.
   a) Find y when $x = 2.8$
   b) Find x when $y = 104.2$
   Give both answers correct to 1 d.p.

10 y is inversely proportional to $\sqrt{x}$ and $y = 3.8$ when $x = 0.17$.
   a) Find y when $x = 0.57$
   b) Find x when $y = 8.7$

11 After a boot sale, takings of £72 are shared between Alice, Sonita and Mia, so that Alice receives $\frac{1}{2}$ of the money, Sonita receives $\frac{2}{3}$ of the remainder and Mia receives the amount left. Find:
   a) the amount Sonita receives
   b) the fraction remaining for Mia.

12 The manager of a function hall calculates the charge per person using the formula:

$$C = \frac{k\sqrt{T}}{n}$$

where T is the number of hours booked, n is the number of people attending and k is a constant.

a) Find k if the cost per person was £2.40 when the hall was booked for 4 hours for a function attended by 80 people.

b) Find the cost per person for a function for 24 people which lasted 9 hours.

c) Rewrite the formula in the form $C = kT^x n^y$, stating the values of x and y.

REVIEW

How much have you learnt?
Tick off each topic in the list when you are confident that you can cope with it.

☐ **Answer questions on ratio and proportion.**

☐ **Work out a percentage of a number.**

☐ **Express one number as a percentage of another.**

☐ **Find the combined percentage increase or decrease.**

☐ **Solve problems involving VAT.**

☐ **Work out problems involving exponential growth or decay.**

☐ **Find constants of proportionality in questions on variation.**

☐ **Simplify ratios.**

Answers

1 21%
2 a) 12 339 chickens b) 6496 cows
3 a) 84.5 km b) 23.7 litres
4 £32.40
5 a) 3 : 2 b) 2 : 3
6 2.5 : 1 and 1 : 0.4
7 16%
8 £180, £210, £60
9 $k = 72.4 \div 5.1^2 = 2.784$
10 a) 21.8 b) $\sqrt{104.2 \div 2.784} = 6.1$
10 $k = 3.8 \times \sqrt{0.17} = 1.57$
11 a) 2.1 b) 0.03
11 a) £24 b) $\frac{1}{6}$
12 a) 96 b) £112.00
12 c) $x = \frac{1}{2}, y = -1$

PREVIEW

By the end of this chapter you will be able to:

- factorise simple algebraic expressions
- rearrange formulae
- solve simultaneous equations algebraically
- solve equations using trial and improvement
- multiply out brackets
- factorise quadratic expressions
- solve quadratic equations
- complete the square
- solve simultaneous equations with a linear and a quadratic expression
- solve inequalities
- simplify and manipulate algebraic fractions
- solve equations from real-life situations
- find the nth terms of sequences
- find the next terms in Fibonacci sequences
- prove statements using algebra.

Things you should know

- Variables are letters such as x or y which are used to represent numbers.
- Expressions are statements involving variables, such as $x^2 + 1$
- An equation is a relationship between expressions with an equals sign in it, such as $x^2 + 1 = 2x$
- A coefficient is a number that multiplies a variable. In the expression $x^2 - 5x$, the coefficient of x^2 is 1 and the coefficient of x is -5

Now try the following questions.

Exercise 3.1

1   Find x where:
   a) $5x + 3 = 23$ **b)** $2x - 5 = 17$
   c) $4 = 16 - 3x$ **d)** $3x + 10 = 4$
   e) $6x - 1 = 2$ **f)** $x + 1 = 11$
   g) $4x + 7 = 2x + 37$ **h)** $x - 1 = 4x - 10$
   i) $2(x - 1) + 5(x + 2) = 57$
   j) $3(1 - x) - 4(2x - 1) = 73$

2   Simplify these.
   a) $\dfrac{3x^2 \times 2x^4}{x^5}$ **b)** $\dfrac{12y^3}{8x^2y}$ **c)** $\dfrac{12y^2}{6y^3}$
   d) $5x^3 + 3x^3 + 2x^2$ **e)** $a(a + b) - b(a - b)$
   f) $b \times (-b^2)$ **g)** $x^2 - 2x(1 - 2x)$
   h) $(x^3)^4$

3   Write the following as single fractions.
   a) $\dfrac{1}{u} + \dfrac{1}{v}$ **b)** $\dfrac{x}{2} + \dfrac{x + 2}{4}$

Answers 3.1

1 a) 4   **b)** 11   **c)** 4   **d)** −2   **e)** 0.5   **f)** 10
   g) −6   **h)** 3   **i)** 7   **j)** −6

2 a) $6x$ **b)** $\dfrac{3y^2}{2x^2}$ **c)** $\dfrac{2}{y}$ or $2y^{-1}$ **d)** $8x^3 + 2x^2$
   e) $a^2 + b^2$ **f)** $-b^3$ **g)** $5x^2 - 2x$ **h)** x^{12}

3 a) $\dfrac{v + u}{uv}$ **b)** $\dfrac{3x + 2}{4}$

Make sure that you can do these questions. If you have trouble with any of them, ask for extra help from your teacher. Ask for some similar questions to try.

The **coefficient** is the number that multiplies the variable. For example, in the expression $2x^2 - x + 4$, the coefficient of x^2 is 2 and the coefficient of x is −1. The 4 is called the **constant**.

Factorising using single brackets

Factorising means splitting a number into its factors. When you factorise, you need to find the highest common factor, i.e. the biggest number or letter that 'goes into' all the terms.

Example 3.1

Factorise $2x + 6$

Solution

Look for the highest common factor of $2x$ and 6; 2 goes in to both terms:

$2(\quad\quad)$

What times 2 makes $2x$? x

What times 2 makes +6? +3

When factorised, $2x + 6 = 2(x + 3)$

Check by expanding out the brackets:

$2(x + 3) = 2x + 6$

Example 3.2

Factorise $x^2 + 5x$

Solution

What goes into both x^2 and $+5x$? x

So write this outside the brackets: $x(\quad\quad)$

x times what makes x^2? x

x times what makes $+5x$? +5

So $x^2 + 5x = x(x + 5)$

Check by expanding out $x(x + 5)$

Example 3.3

Factorise $y^2 - y$

Solution

What goes into both y^2 and $-y$? y

So write $y($ $)$

y times what makes y^2? y

y times what makes $-y$? -1

So $y^2 - y = y(y - 1)$

Example 3.4

Factorise fully $12c^2 - 16c$

Solution

What goes into both $12c^2$ and $-16c$?

4 goes into 12 and 16, c goes into c^2 and c.

So $4c$ goes into both $12c^2$ and $-16c$ (i.e. it is the highest common factor of $12c^2$ and $-16c$).

So write $4c($ $)$

$4c$ times what makes $12c^2$? $3c$

$4c$ times what makes $-16c$? -4

So $12c^2 - 16c = 4c(3c - 4)$

Example 3.5

Factorise fully $x^2y + xy^2$

Solution

What goes in to both $x^2y + xy^2$? x and y, or xy

So write $xy($ $)$

xy times what makes x^2y? x

xy times what makes $+xy^2$? $+y$

So $x^2y + xy^2 = xy(x + y)$

Example 3.6

Factorise fully $9d^3 - 3d^2$

Solution

The highest common factor of $9d^3$ and $-3d^2$ is $3d^2$.

$3d^2$ times what makes $9d^3$? $3d$

$3d^2$ times what makes $-3d^2$? -1

So $9d^3 - 3d^2 = 3d^2(3d - 1)$

Exercise 3.2

Factorise fully the following expressions:

1 $12x - 4$ **2** $x^2 + 7x$

3 $4x^2 - 6x$ **4** $6y^3 + 9y^2$

5 $16ab + 10bc$ **6** $4c^2 - 2ac$

7 $10a^2b^2 - 5a$

Answers 3.2

7 $5a(2ab^2 - 1)$

6 $2c(2c - a)$

5 $2b(8a + 5c)$

4 $3y^2(2y + 3)$

3 $2x(2x - 3)$

2 $x(x + 7)$

1 $4(3x - 1)$

Formula rearrangement

When rearranging a formula, follow these simple rules.

- You can move a constant from one side to the other. In doing so, its sign changes. So moving $+2$ to the other side makes it -2.

- You can multiply or divide by any number, as long as you do it to every term on both sides.

- If the required term is negative, e.g. $-6x$, you can take it over to the other side, as $6x$.

Linear equations

The subject appears once

Example 3.7

Make x the subject of the formula $y = mx + c$

Solution

The term in x is positive, so leave it where it is.

$y = \boxed{mx} + c$

Take the c over to the other side, making it $-c$.

$y - c = \boxed{mx}$

Divide everything on both sides of the equation by m.

$$\frac{y - c}{m} = x$$

$$x = \frac{y - c}{m}$$

Example 3.8

Make y the subject of the formula $ab - ky = c$

Solution

The term in y is negative, so move it to the other side of the equation. It becomes positive on the other side.

$ab = c + ky$

Now move the '+c' across to the other side, where it becomes $-c$.

$ab - c = ky$

At the moment, y is multiplied by k.
Divide everything on both sides by k.

$\dfrac{ab - c}{k} = y$ or $y = \dfrac{ab - c}{k}$

The required subject appears twice

Example 3.9

Rearrange $2hx = kx + m$ to make x the subject of the formula.

Solution

Take both terms with x to one side of the equation.

$2hx - kx = m$

Now factorise the left-hand side.

$x(2h - k) = m$

Divide both sides by the term in the brackets.

$x = \dfrac{m}{2h - k}$

Example 3.10

Make r the subject of the formula $rh - A = \pi rl$

Solution

The equation has two terms in r:

$rh - A = \pi rl$

Take them to one side of the equation.

$rh - A - \pi rl = 0$ or $-A = \pi rl - rh$

Take all terms not containing r over to the other side.

$rh - \pi rl = A$ or $-A = \pi rl - rh$

Now factorise:

$r(h - \pi l) = A$ or $-A = r(\pi l - h)$

Then divide everything on both sides by the coefficient of r.

$r = \dfrac{A}{h - \pi l}$ or $r = \dfrac{-A}{\pi l - h}$

The required subject appears in the denominator

Example 3.11

Make x the subject of the formula $b + \dfrac{1}{x} = a$

Solution

Multiply everything by x (including b).

$bx + 1 = ax$

Take the two terms containing x to the same side of the equation (the term without x goes to the other side).

Either $bx - ax = -1$ or $1 = ax - bx$

Take out the common factor, x, leaving either $(b - a)$ or $(a - b)$ in brackets.

$x(b - a) = -1$ or $1 = x(a - b)$

Divide both sides by the term in brackets.

$x = \dfrac{-1}{b - a}$ or $x = \dfrac{1}{a - b}$

Equations with powers and roots

Example 3.12

Rearrange $v^2 = u^2 - 2as$ to make u the subject of the formula.

Solution

As the term in u is positive, leave it where it is,

$v^2 = u^2 - 2as$

and take the $2as$ over to the other side:

$v^2 + 2as = u^2$

Now take the square root of everything on both sides.

$\pm\sqrt{v^2 + 2as} = u$

When square rooting, a ± should be written before the root sign on one side of the equation.

Example 3.13

Make e the subject of this formula.

$b = \dfrac{c}{e} - f$

Solution

Start by taking the f to the other side.

$b + f = \dfrac{c}{e}$

Now, because the required subject is on the bottom, i.e. dividing, multiply both sides by e:

$e(b + f) = c$

Now divide both sides by $(b + f)$:

$e = \dfrac{c}{b + f}$

Example 3.14

Rewrite the formula $T = 2\pi\sqrt{\dfrac{l}{g}}$ to give l in terms of T and g.

Solution

Divide both sides by 2π.

$$\frac{T}{2\pi} = \sqrt{\frac{l}{g}}$$

Now square both sides:

$$\left(\frac{T}{2\pi}\right)^2 = \frac{l}{g}$$

Multiply both sides by g.

$$g\left(\frac{T}{2\pi}\right)^2 = l \quad \text{or} \quad \frac{gT^2}{4\pi^2} = l$$

Be careful when squaring or finding the square root:

$(2\pi)^2 = 4\pi^2$, **not** $2\pi^2$

$(x + y)^2$ is **not** the same as $x^2 + y^2$

$\sqrt{x^2 + y^2}$ is **not** the same as $x + y$

Exercise 3.3

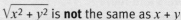

Rewrite the following equations in terms of the variable in brackets.

1 $d = b - ac$ (c)

2 $uv = 2v + w$ (v)

3 $a = \dfrac{b}{c} + d$ (c)

4 $V = 2 - \pi rhl$ (h)

5 $s = ut + \frac{1}{2}at^2$ (a)

6 $y = \dfrac{3x}{x - 2}$ (x)

7 $A = \pi r\sqrt{u + v}$ (u)

8 $\dfrac{1}{x} + b = a$ (x)

Answers 3.3

1 $c = \dfrac{b-d}{a}$ 2 $v = \dfrac{w}{u-2}$

3 $c = \dfrac{b}{a-d}$ 4 $h = \dfrac{2-V}{\pi rl}$

5 $a = \dfrac{2s-2ut}{t^2}$ 6 $x = \dfrac{2y}{y-3}$ or $\dfrac{-2y}{3-y}$

7 $u = \left(\dfrac{A}{\pi r}\right)^2 - v$ 8 $x = \dfrac{1}{a-b}$ or $\dfrac{1}{a-b}$

Rearranging formulae to help solve problems

Example 3.15

The manager of a leisure centre is having some refurbishment done. The carpenter contracted to re-floor the squash courts states that he charges £35.00 initial call-out fee, plus £15.00 per hour worked. Using C to represent the cost in pounds, and h to represent the hours worked, the manager works out the following equation for the total cost of carpentry: $C = 35 + 15h$.

The plumber contracted to renovate the shower rooms charges £50.00 initial call-out fee plus £35.00 per hour worked.

a) Write the equation for the total plumbing cost.

b) Find the number of hours worked if the bill for plumbing is £645.00.

Solution

a) The equation for the total plumbing cost is $C = 50 + 35h$

b) To find the number of hours worked, rearrange the formula to give h in terms of C.

$$\frac{C - 50}{35} = h$$

Replacing C by 645 gives the answer 17 hours.

Even if the question doesn't directly ask you to rearrange the formula, it's often easier to do so before putting the numbers in.

Example 3.16

Sarah is trying to get a good crop of tomatoes on her allotment. First she measures 2 litres of water into a watering can and then she adds 0.5 litres of liquid fertiliser for every further litre of water. If the can holds 8 litres, how much fertiliser has she used when the can is full?

Solution

Write the information in the form of an equation. You could use T to represent the total amount of liquid, W to represent the amount of water added after the initial 2 litres, and f to represent the amount of fertiliser added, all in litres. The equation is:

$T = 2 + W + f$

You are told that $f = 0.5W$, so $W = 2f$. You want to find f, so replace W:

$T = 2 + 3f$

Rearranging the information gives

$$f = \frac{T - 2}{3}$$

Substituting $T = 8$ gives the answer $f = 2$.

2 litres of fertiliser have been used.

Exercise 3.4

1 An IT consultant requested 25% of the first year's profits of a new business that he had advised on, plus £2000 expenses. If P is the first year's profits and S is his share,

a) write a formula for S to show how the consultant can work out the amount he should receive,

b) rewrite the formula making P the subject,

c) work out what the first year's profits of the business were if the IT consultant received £39 500 for his part.

2 The formula for the volume of a triangular based pyramid is $\frac{1}{3}Ah$ where A is the area of the base and h is the height of the triangle.

a) Rewrite the equation $V = \frac{1}{3}Ah$ to give h in terms of V and A.

b) Hence or otherwise find the height of a triangular based pyramid of volume $977.16\,\text{cm}^3$ and base area $95.8\,\text{cm}^2$.

Answers 3.4

1 a) $S = 0.25P + 2000$

b) $P = \dfrac{S - 2000}{0.25}$

c) $P = \dfrac{39\,500 - 2000}{0.25} = £150\,000$

2 a) It may be easier to start by writing $V = \dfrac{Ah}{3}$

Then $3V = Ah$

and so $h = \dfrac{3V}{A}$

b) $h = \dfrac{3 \times 977.16}{95.8} = 30.6\,\text{cm}$

 TAKE A BREAK

You've worked hard and you deserve a break.

Simultaneous equations

These are two equations involving two variables (usually x and y) and you need to find the values of x and y that satisfy both equations.

With simultaneous equations you need to find x and y, so: Simultaneous Equations are SEXY.

Remember *that the* ***coefficient*** *is the number multiplying a variable. For example, in the expression $x^2 - 2x - 1$ the coefficient of x^2 is 1, the coefficient of x is -2 and the constant is -1.*

Algebraic solution

There are two ways of solving simultaneous equations using algebra – elimination and substitution.

Method 1 – Elimination

This is the most common method. It is used when all the variables are on the same side of the equations.

Example 3.17

Solve the following simultaneous equations.

$$4x + 2y = 22 \qquad 3x + 2y = 19$$

Solution

1 One variable must have the same coefficient in both equations (ignoring whether they are positive or negative). There is a $2y$ in both.

2 If the signs are the same, you take away one equation from the other.
If the signs are opposite you add (plus) them.

Remember: STOP
      Same **T**ake, **O**pposite **P**lus

3 Both $2y$ terms are positive (same sign), so take away. Box the terms that will cancel out.

$$4x + 2y = 22$$
$$3x + 2y = 19$$
$$\overline{x = 3} \qquad (4x - 3x = x,\ 22 - 19 = 3)$$

4 Now use the easier equation to find y.

$$3x + 2y = 19$$
$$9 + 2y = 19 \qquad (\text{because } 3x = 3 \times 3 = 9)$$
$$2y = 10$$
$$y = 5$$

Check using the other equation ($4x + 2y = 22$).

$$4 \times 3 + 2 \times 5 = 22$$

Example 3.18

Solve these simultaneous equations.

$5x - 2y = 36$ **1**

$3x - 2y = 16$ **2**

Solution

Using STOP, subtract equation **2** from equation **1**.

$5x - 2y = 36$

$3x - 2y = 16$

$2x \quad = 20$ (because $-2y - -2y = -2y + 2y = 0$)

$\quad x \quad = 10$

Substitute $x = 10$ into equation **2**.

$30 - 2y = 16$

$30 - 16 = 2y$

$\quad 14 = 2y$ so $y = 7$

Check in equation **1** $\quad 30 - 14 = 16$

This is true, so the answers for x and y are true.

Example 3.19

Solve these equations.

$3x + 2y = 16$ **1** $\qquad x + y = 5$ **2**

Solution

1 Ignoring the signs, are the coefficients of either variable the same? No. So multiply the equation with the lower coefficient to make the coefficients of either x or y the same (ignoring signs). To eliminate y, multiply the second equation by 2. (If eliminating x, you would have to multiply it by 3.)

$3x + 2y = 16$ **1**

$2x + 2y = 10$ **2** $\times$ 2

$\quad x \quad = 6$

*Using **STOP**, subtract as the signs of the y-terms are the same.*

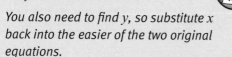

You also need to find y, so substitute x back into the easier of the two original equations.

$x + y = 5$

$6 + y = 5$

$\quad y = -1$

Check in equation **1** $\quad 3 \times 6 + 2 \times -1 = 16$

Sometimes you have to multiply both equations to get the same coefficient in x or y. If the equations were:

$2x + 3y = 5$ **1** $\qquad 3x - 5y = 2$ **2**

you could multiply **1** by 3 and **2** by 2 to get $6x$ in both, or you could multiply **1** by 5 and **2** by 3 to get $15y$ in both. If you go for $6x$ in both, you then subtract the equations (**S**ame **T**ake). If you decide to use $15y$ you add the equations (**O**pposite **P**lus). If you have a choice, it's usually easier to add.

Example 3.20

Solve these equations.

$5x - 4y = 32$ $\qquad 3x + 4y = 0$

Solution

Ignoring the signs, the coefficients of y are the same.

***STOP** **S**ame **T**ake, **O**pposite **P**lus*

The signs are opposite for the $4y$ terms so add the equations. ($-4y + 4y = 0$ so y is eliminated.)

$5x - 4y = 32$

$3x + 4y = 0$

$8x \quad = 32$

$\quad x \quad = 4$

Now find y.

Use the simpler second equation, $3x + 4y = 0$.

$12 + 4y = 0$

$\quad 4y = -12$

$\quad y = -3$

Check in the first equation, $5x - 4y = 32$.

$5 \times 4 - 4 \times -3 = 32$

Exercise 3.5

Solve the following simultaneous equations.

1 $3x + 2y = 31$ $\qquad$ **2** $12x - 5y = 79$

$\quad x + 2y = 21$ $\qquad\qquad 9x + 5y = 68$

3 $5x + 4y = 38$ $\qquad$ **4** $6x + 5y = 31$

$\quad 3x + 5y = 41$ $\qquad\qquad 3x + 4y = 23$

5 $5x - 3y = 12$ $\qquad$ **6** $10x - 7y = 26$

$\quad 2x - 3y = 6$ $\qquad\qquad 2x - 7y = 22$

Answers 3.5

5 $x = 2, y = -\frac{2}{3}$ $\qquad$ **6** $x = \frac{1}{2}, y = -3$

3 $x = 2, y = 7$ $\qquad$ **4** $x = 1, y = 5$

1 $x = 5, y = 8$ $\qquad$ **2** $x = 7, y = 1$

Method 2 – Substitution

Use this method when x and y are on different sides in at least one equation.

Example 3.21

Solve these equations.

$5x - 3y = 5$ **1**

$x = y - 3$ **2**

Solution

We can solve this by simply replacing the x in the first equation by $y - 3$ from the second equation, remembering to bracket it.

$5(y - 3) - 3y = 5$

$5y - 15 - 3y = 5$

$2y - 15 = 5$

$2y = 20$

$y = 10$

Using **2**:

$x = 10 - 3$

$x = 7$

Check in **1** $5 \times 7 - 3 \times 10 = 5$

Exercise 3.6

Solve these simultaneous equations.

1 $5x + 3y = 27$ **2** $5x - y = 15$

      $y = x - 7$ $y = 2x - 9$

3 $4x - 3y = -1$ **4** $2y - x = 3$

      $y = 2x - 1$ $x = 1 - 2y$

Answers 3.6

1 $x = 6, y = -1$ **2** $x = 2, y = -5$

3 $x = 2, y = 3$ **4** $x = -1, y = 1$

 TAKE A BREAK

Time for another break. This chapter is quite challenging. Don't try to rush it.

Trial and improvement

This is a method of finding a solution to an equation by substituting numbers into a given formula until you find one that is the solution to the required level of accuracy.

Example 3.22

Find the solution near $x = 3$ to the equation $x^3 + 2x = 44$ to one decimal place.

Solution

Firstly create a table for x and the left-hand side of the formula

in this case $x^3 + 2x$:

x	$x^3 + 2x$	Comments
3	$3^3 + 2 \times 3 = 33$	Too low

This answer is less than 44, so try a number slightly larger, such as 3.5:

3.5	$3.5^3 + 2 \times 3.5 = 49.875$	Too high

This is too big, so try a smaller number, say 3.3:

3.3	42.537	Too low

Try 3.4:

3.4	46.104	Too high

The x-value that will give an answer of 44 is somewhere between 3.3 and 3.4. Correct to 1 decimal place, the answer will be either 3.3 or 3.4. To find out which one it is, substitute the number halfway between these two numbers, 3.35:

3.35	44.295	

This is too high, so the x-value that gives an answer of 44 lies between 3.3 and 3.35. This would round to 3.3 (to 1 d.p.), so the answer is $x = 3.3$.

You must follow this process to get full marks.

Example 3.23

Find the solution of $2x^3 - x = 400$ to two decimal places. Start with the value $x = 6$.

Solution

x	$2x^3 - x$	Comments
6	426	Too high
5.8	384.424	Too low
5.9	404.858	Too high
5.87	398.654	Too low
5.88	400.715	Too high

So the value of x that satisfies the equation lies somewhere between 5.87 and 5.88. So substitute the number halfway between these values, 5.875

5.875	399.683 ...	Too low

So the solution must lie between 5.875 and 5.88, which rounds to 5.88 to 2 decimal places.

Exercise 3.7

Use trial and improvement to solve the following equations correct to 2 decimal places.

1 $3x^3 + 7x = 89$ Start with $x = 3$

2 $x^3 + 3x = 103$ Start with $x = 4$

Multiplying out (expanding) double brackets

*We use **FOIL** – **F**irst **O**uter **I**nner **L**ast to expand double brackets. Use your own method if you prefer.*

Example 3.24

Expand these brackets. $(x + 1)(2x + 3)$

Solution

Using FOIL

	First	Outer	Inner	Last
	↓	↓	↓	↓
$(x + 1)(2x + 3)$	$= 2x^2$	$+ 3x$	$+ 2x$	$+ 3$
	$= 2x^2 + 5x + 3$			

A common mistake is to add the last terms instead of multiplying.

Exercise 3.8

Expand the following.

1 $(x + 3)(x - 2)$ 2 $(x - 1)(x + 1)$ 3 $(4 - x)(x + 7)$
4 $(2x - 1)(3x - 5)$ 5 $(2x - 5)^2$

Quadratic expressions

Factorising into two brackets

Factorising when the coefficient of x^2 is 1

Type 1: the constant term is positive, so factors have the same sign.

Type 1a: the x-term is positive, so both terms are positive.

Example 3.25

Factorise $x^2 + 7x + 12$

Solution

List all the pairs of factors of the constant term. The correct pair sums to the coefficient of the x-term.

$x^2 + 7x + 12$	+12	+6	+4
	+1	+2	+3
	+13	+8	+7

$= (x + 4)(x + 3)$

Type 1: the constant term is positive, so factors have the same sign.

Type 1b: the x-term is negative, so both terms are negative.

Example 3.26

Factorise $x^2 - 14x + 40$

Solution

$x^2 - 14x + 40$	−40	−20	−10	−8
	−1	−2	−4	−5
	−41	−22	−14	−13

$= (x - 10)(x - 4)$

Type 2: the constant term is negative, so the signs are different.

Type 2a: the x-term is positive, so the larger factor is positive.

Example 3.27

Factorise $x^2 + 4x - 45$

Solution

$x^2 + 4x - 45$	+45	+15	+9
	−1	−3	−5
	+44	+12	+4

$= (x + 9)(x - 5)$

Type 2: the constant term is negative, so the signs are different.

Type 2b: the x-term is negative, so the larger factor is negative.

Example 3.28

Factorise $x^2 - 7x - 60$

Solution

$x^2 - 7x - 60$	−60	−30	−20	−15	−12	−10
	+1	+2	+3	+4	+5	+6
	−59	−28	−17	−11	−7	−4

$= (x - 12)(x + 5)$

Exercise 3.9

Factorise the following expressions.

1 $x^2 - x - 12$ 2 $x^2 - 9x + 8$
3 $x^2 + 2x - 15$ 4 $x^2 + 10x + 24$
5 $x^2 - 2x - 48$ 6 $x^2 - 12x + 35$

J u s t   t o   r e c a p . . .

1 Start by looking at the sign of the constant.

2 If it is positive, both brackets have the same sign. If it is negative the brackets will have different signs.

3 Check your answer by expanding out the brackets.

A summary of factorisation

... when the coefficient of x^2 is 1

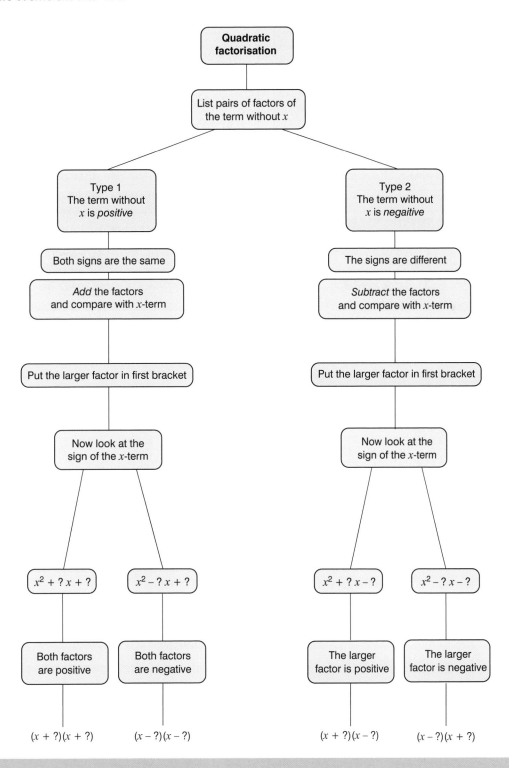

TAKE A BREAK

Further quadratic expressions

Factorising when the coefficient of x^2 is greater than 1

Example 3.29

Factorise $3x^2 + 13x - 10$

Solution

The term in x^2 can only be the product of $3x$ and x. So write these at the start of the brackets.

$(3x\ \ )(x\ \ )$

Now write all the pairs of numbers with product 10:
$1 \times 10; 2 \times 5$.

Experiment to see which makes the coefficient of x equal to 13.

$3x^2 + 13x - 10 = (3x - 2)(x + 5)$

Exercise 3.10

Factorise the following expressions.

1 $5x^2 - 7x - 6$ 2 $3x^2 + x - 10$

3 $2x^2 - 11x + 12$ 4 $3x^2 + 11x + 6$

5 $2x^2 + x - 10$ 6 $4x^2 + 4x + 1$

Answers 3.10

1 $(5x + 3)(x - 2)$ 2 $(3x - 5)(x + 2)$
3 $(2x - 3)(x - 4)$ 4 $(3x + 2)(x + 3)$
5 $(2x + 5)(x - 2)$ 6 $(2x + 1)^2$

Factorising in pairs

This is an alternative method of factorising quadratics. To factorise $ax^2 + bx + c$, find two numbers which have a product of ac and a sum of b, split the term x up into two terms using these two numbers as coefficients, then factorise in two pairs, then factorise again.

Example 3.30

a) Factorise $6x^2 + 7x - 20$

b) Solve $6x^2 + 7x - 20 = 0$

Solution

a) $ac = -120$ $b = 7$
15 and -8 have a product of -120 and a sum of 7, so split up $7x$ into
$15x - 8x$ (or $-8x + 15x$):

$6x^2 + 7x - 20 = 6x^2 + 15x - 8x - 20$

then factorise in pairs, ensuring that the expressions in the brackets are the same:

$= 3x(2x + 5) - 4(2x + 5)$

next factorise out the expression in the brackets:

$= (2x + 5)(3x - 4)$

[If you cannot see how this line has been found from the previous line, substitute $y = 2x + 5$ to give $3xy - 4y$ which factorises to $y(3x - 4) = (2x + 5)(3x - 4)$]

b) Start by factorising the quadratic:
$(2x + 5)(3x - 4) = 0$
Now remember that if the product of two expressions is zero, then one or both of the expressions must also equal zero. Equate each of the two expressions inside the brackets to zero:

$2x + 5 = 0$ $3x - 4 = 0$

$x = \dfrac{-5}{2}$ $x = \dfrac{4}{3}$

The same method can also be used for the type of expression in the example below.

Example 3.31

Factorise $pq - p + q^2 - q$

Solution

Factorise $pq - p$ and $+ q^2 - q$ separately. Factorise each of the two expressions, making the term inside each pair of brackets the same.

$pq - p + q^2 - q = p(q - 1) + q(q - 1) = (q - 1)(p + q)$

Exercise 3.11

1 Factorise $x^2 - 2x - xy + 2y$

2 Using the method of factorising in pairs, or otherwise, factorise then solve these equations.
   a) $30x^2 - 37x + 10 = 0$
   b) $32x^2 - 4x - 21 = 0$

Answers 3.11

1. Factorising the first pair of terms gives $x^2 - 2x = x(x-2)$. Factorise the second pair of terms, making sure that $(x - 2)$ is left inside the brackets: $-xy + 2y = -y(x - 2)$
$x^2 - 2x - xy + 2y = x(x - 2) - y(x - 2)$
$= (x - 2)(x - y)$

2. a) $(5x - 2)(6x - 5) = 0$, $x = \frac{2}{5}, \frac{5}{6}$
   b) $(4x + 3)(8x - 7) = 0$, $x = -\frac{3}{4}, \frac{7}{8}$

Quadratic formula

The formula for the solution of the general quadratic $ax^2 + bx + c = 0$ is

$$x = \frac{-b \pm \sqrt{b^2 - 4ac}}{2a}$$

Make sure that the equation is in the form $ax^2 + bx + c = 0$ before using the formula, e.g.

$3x^2 - 2x = 2 \Rightarrow 3x^2 - 2x - 2 = 0$

$7 + \frac{3}{x} = 2x \Rightarrow 7x + 3 = 2x^2 \Rightarrow 2x^2 - 7x - 3 = 0$

Exercise 3.12

Solve $5x^2 + 6x - 10 = 0$ to 2 d.p.

Answers 3.12

$a = 5$, $b = 6$ and $c = -10$

$$x = \frac{-6 \pm \sqrt{(6)^2 - 4(5)(-10)}}{2(5)}$$

Firstly simplify the expressions inside the square root and the denominator:

$$x = \frac{-6 \pm \sqrt{236}}{10}$$

Calculate the numerator then divide by the denominator: $x = 0.94, -2.14$

Difference of two squares

These are quadratic expressions, but they have no term in x, and the two terms are separated by a minus sign.

A general form of the difference of two squares is $x^2 - y^2$

Draw two pairs of empty brackets next to each other:
( )( )

To factorise, square root the first term and write it inside both pairs of brackets at the beginning:

$(x \quad)(x \quad)$

Then square root the second term and put it at the end of both pairs of brackets:

$(x \quad y)(x \quad y)$

Between the terms, put a '+' in one pair of brackets and a '−' in the other:

$(x + y)(x - y)$

So $x^2 - y^2 = (x + y)(x - y)$

Example 3.32

Factorise the following expressions:

a) $x^2 - 4$ b) $a^2 - b^2$

c) $y^2 - 9d^2$ d) $2x^2 - 50$

e) $x^2 - 1$ f) $100x^2 - 49y^2$

Solution

a) $(x + 2)(x - 2)$

b) $(a + b)(a - b)$

c) $(y + 3d)(y - 3d)$

d) First take out the common factor, 2:
$2(x^2 - 25) = 2(x + 5)(x - 5)$

e) $(x + 1)(x - 1)$

f) $(10x + 7y)(10x - 7y)$

Example 3.33

a) Factorise $x^2 - 16$.

b) Hence or otherwise solve $x^2 - 16 = 0$.

Solution

a) $(x + 4)(x - 4)$

b) The word 'Hence' in the question implies that your answer to **a)** will help you to answer this part.

$(x + 4)(x - 4) = 0$

$x + 4 = 0$ or $x - 4 = 0$

$x = -4, 4$

The 'otherwise' method: $x^2 = 16$

$x = 4, -4$

***Remember** that when you square root, there are two possible answers: one positive and one negative.*

Example 3.34

a) Factorise $x^2 - y^2$

b) Without using a calculator, evaluate $321^2 - 221^2$.

Solution

a) $(x + y)(x - y)$

b) $(321 + 221)(321 - 221) = 542 \times 100 = 54200$

This is much easier than squaring 321 and 221 and then finding the difference.

Be ready for this if it is on the non-calculator paper.

Exercise 3.13

1 Factorise the following expressions:

a) $x^2 - 25$ b) $c^2 - 36$

c) $y^2 - 49d^2$ d) $3x^2 - 48$

2 a) Factorise $x^2 - 64$.

b) Hence or otherwise solve $x^2 - 64 = 0$.

3 a) Factorise $x^2 - y^2$.

b) Without using a calculator, evaluate $348^2 - 338^2$.

Answers 3.13

b) $(348 + 338)(348 - 338) = 686 \times 10 = 6860$

3 a) $(x + y)(x - y)$

2 a) $(x + 8)(x - 8)$ b) $x = -8, 8$

d) First take out the common factor, 3:
$3(x^2 - 16) = 3(x + 4)(x - 4)$

c) $(y + 7d)(y - 7d)$

1 a) $(x + 5)(x - 5)$ b) $(c + 6)(c - 6)$

Solving quadratic equations

Quadratic equations are of the form
$ax^2 + bx + c = 0.$

For example, $2x^2 + x - 4 = 0$ is a quadratic equation.

Solution of quadratic equations

The most common ways of solving quadratic equations for GCSE are as follows:

1 factorising

2 quadratic formula

3 graphically (see Chapter 4, Graphs for this method).

4 completing the square (see the next section for this method).

Solution of quadratics – method 1

After taking all terms on to one side and factorising, equate each bracket to zero and solve.

For example $x^2 + 6x + 5 = 0$

$$(x + 5)(x + 1) = 0$$

When the product of two numbers is zero, one or the other must be zero.

So either $x + 5 = 0$ or $x + 1 = 0$

$x = -5$ $x = -1$

You must have a zero on the right-hand side of the equation to use this method.

Also, if you have a negative coefficient of x^2, take all terms on to the other side of the equation to make the coefficient positive.

Solving $6 - x^2 - 10x = 0$ is the same as solving $0 = x^2 + 10x - 6$.

Solution of quadratics – method 2

You may have to use the formula for solving quadratics.

$$x = \frac{-b \pm \sqrt{b^2 - 4ac}}{2a}$$

Don't worry, you do not need to learn this – it'll be on the *Information and formulae sheet* of your exam paper.

Use this method if:

• the question asks you to give your answer to a certain number of decimal places

• the equation looks difficult to factorise.

Exercise 3.14

1 Find the values of x which satisfy these equations.

a) $x^2 + 8x = -15$ b) $2x^2 - 11x + 5 = 0$

c) $x^2 + 24x = 25$ d) $x^2 - 9 = 0$

e) $x^2 = 25$

2 Find the values of x in the following questions, correct to two decimal places.

a) $3x^2 - 11x + 4 = 0$ b) $4x^2 - 17x + 1 = 0$

c) $2x^2 + 8x = 3$ d) $3x^2 + 1 = 9x$

e) $6 - x^2 - 10x = 0$

Answers 3.14

e) $x = -10.57, x = 0.57$

c) $x = 0.35, x = -4.35$ **d)** $x = 0.12, x = 2.88$

2 a) $x = 3.26, x = 0.41$ **b)** $x = 4.19, x = 0.06$

e) $x = -5, x = 5$

c) $x = -25, x = 1$ **d)** $x = -3, x = 3$

1 a) $x = -5, x = -3$ **b)** $x = 0.5, x = 5$

 TAKE A BREAK

Definitely time for another break!
There's a bit more hard work coming up.

Completing the square

Completing the square is a method of rewriting a quadratic equation. When written in this format, you can find the points where the graph crosses the x-axis (i.e. the solutions to the equation).

For the quadratic expression $x^2 + bx + c$, the completed square form is $(x + p)^2 + q$

Before you start

Check that you can expand the following:
1 $(x + 3)^2$
2 $(x - 2)^2$
3 $(x + 4)^2$
4 $(x - 6)^2$
5 $(x + p)^2$

Answers

1 $x^2 + 6x + 9$
2 $x^2 - 4x + 4$
3 $x^2 + 8x + 16$
4 $x^2 - 12x + 36$
5 $x^2 + 2px + p^2$

The coefficient of x is twice the number inside the brackets.

To find p in the completed square form $(x + p)^2 + q$, a simple method is to divide the coefficient of x by 2. Then subtract the square of this number outside the brackets:

$x^2 + 8x = (x + 4)^2 - 16$

$x^2 - 10x = (x - 5)^2 - 25$

$x^2 + 2x = (x + 1)^2 - 1$

$x^2 - 6x = (x - 3)^2 - 9$

The following quadratic expressions have been written in completed square form using this method:

$x^2 + 4x + 7 = (x + 2)^2 - 4 + 7 = (x + 2)^2 + 3$

$x^2 + 8x + 10 = (x + 4)^2 - 16 + 10 = (x + 4)^2 - 6$

$x^2 - 12x + 32 = (x - 6)^2 - 36 + 32 = (x - 6)^2 - 4$

$x^2 - 6x + 8 = (x - 3)^2 - 9 + 8 = (x - 3)^2 - 1$

An alternative method of finding the completed square form is to write the given quadratic equal to $(x + p)^2 + q$, and expand this expression. Equate the coefficients of x to find p, then equate the constant terms (i.e. the terms not involving x) and find q.

Example 3.35

Write the following expressions in completed square form.

a) $x^2 + 8x + 11$ **b)** $x^2 - 4x + 1$

Solution

a) $x^2 + 8x + 11 = (x + p)^2 + q$
$\qquad\qquad\quad = x^2 + 2px + p^2 + q$

Equating coefficients of x: $2p = 8 \Rightarrow p = 4$

Equating constant terms: $p^2 + q = 11$
$\qquad\qquad\qquad\qquad 4^2 + q = 11$
$\qquad\qquad\qquad\qquad\quad q = -5$

$x^2 + 8x + 11 = (x + 4)^2 - 5$

b) $x^2 - 4x + 1 = (x + p)^2 + q$
$\qquad\qquad\quad = x^2 + 2px + p^2 + q$

Equating coefficients of x: $2p = -4 \Rightarrow p = -2$

Equating constant terms: $p^2 + q = 1$
$\qquad\qquad\qquad (-2)^2 + q = 1 \Rightarrow q = -3$

When squaring negative numbers on your calculator, remember to put them in brackets.

$x^2 - 4x + 1 = (x - 2)^2 - 3$

Finding the turning point of a quadratic written in completed square form as $y = (x + p)^2 + q$

The minimum value of $(x + p)^2$ is zero. So the minimum value of $(x + p)^2 + q$ is q.

This occurs when $x + p = 0$, or when $x = -p$.

Therefore the coordinates of the turning point (minimum) of $y = (x + p)^2 + q$ are $(-p, q)$.

For example, the coordinates of the turning point of $y = (x + 3)^2 - 4$ are $(-3, -4)$, and those of $y = (x - 7)^2 + 6$ are $(7, 6)$.

Exercise 3.15

Write the following quadratic expressions in completed square form. Hence write down the minimum value of the expression and the value of x at which it occurs.

a) $x^2 - 10x + 30$ **b)** $x^2 + 2x - 5$

c) $x^2 - 6x + 7$ **d)** $x^2 + 3x + 4$

Answers 3.15

a) $(x - 5)^2 + 5$
Minimum value 5 when $x = 5$

b) $(x + 1)^2 - 6$
Minimum value −6 when $x = -1$

c) $(x - 3)^2 - 2$
Minimum value −2 when $x = 3$

d) $(x + 1.5)^2 + 1.75$
Minimum value 1.75 when $x = -1.5$

Solving a quadratic equation in completed square form

For the equation, $(x - r)^2 - s = 0$
take the s over to the other side $(x - r)^2 = s$
then square root (remember the ±) $x - r = \pm\sqrt{s}$
take the r over, putting it in front of the $\pm\sqrt{s}$
$$x = r \pm \sqrt{s}$$

Example 3.36

Write the following quadratic equations in completed square form, then solve. Write your answers as exact numbers.

a) $x^2 + 8x + 9 = 0$

b) $x^2 - 6x + 4 = 0$

Solution

a) $(x + 4)^2 - 7 = 0$

$x + 4 = \pm\sqrt{7}$

$x = -4 \pm \sqrt{7}$

These, written in surd form, are the exact answers.

b) $(x - 3)^2 - 5 = 0$

$x - 3 = \pm\sqrt{5}$

$x = 3 \pm \sqrt{5}$

Exercise 3.16

1 Write the following quadratic equation in completed square form, then solve. Write your answers in exact form.

$x^2 + 2x - 1 = 0$

2 Write the following quadratic equation in completed square form, then solve. Give your answers to 2 decimal places.

$x^2 - 12x + 29 = 0$

Answers 3.16

1 $(x + 1)^2 - 2 = 0$
$x = -1 \pm \sqrt{2}$

2 $(x - 6)^2 - 7 = 0$
$x = 6 \pm \sqrt{7}$
$x = 3.35, 8.65$

Simultaneous equations with one linear and one quadratic equation

Rearrange the linear equation to make one variable the subject.

Then substitute this in to the quadratic equation using brackets, expand and solve by factorisation, using the formula or completing the square.

Put the substituted expression in brackets!

Example 3.37

Solve the following simultaneous equations:

$x + 2y = 2$ $x^2 + 2y^2 = 18$

Solution

Rearrange the first equation to make x the value (this gives the easier right-hand side):

$x = 2 - 2y$

Substitute $2 - 2y$ in place of x in the second equation:

$(2 - 2y)^2 + 2y^2 = 18$

Put the substituted expression in brackets!

$4 - 8y + 4y^2 + 2y^2 = 18$

$6y^2 - 8y - 14 = 0$

Divide through by 2:

$3y^2 - 4y - 7 = 0$

$(3y - 7)(y + 1) = 0$

$$y = \frac{7}{3}, -1$$

When $y = \frac{7}{3}$, $x = 2 - 2 \times \frac{7}{3} = -\frac{8}{3}$

When $y = -1$, $x = 2 - 2 \times -1 = 4$

If you have time in the exam, check that your answers satisfy both equations.

Example 3.38

Solve the following simultaneous equations, giving your answers to 2 decimal places.

$3x - 4y = 7$

$5x^2 - 2y = 9$

Solution

Rearrange the linear equation, making y the subject (choose y because this is easier to substitute into the second equation):

From the linear equation, $y = \dfrac{3x - 7}{4}$

Substitute this into the second equation, putting the expression in brackets:

$$5x^2 - 2\left(\frac{3x - 7}{4}\right) = 9$$

Cancel the 2 with the 4: $\quad 5x^2 - \dfrac{3x - 7}{2} = 9$

Multiply through by 2: $\quad 10x^2 - (3x - 7) = 18$

Expand, multiplying the terms in the brackets by -1:

$$10x^2 - 3x + 7 = 18$$

Simplify: $\quad 10x^2 - 3x - 11 = 0$

As the question asks you to write the answers to 2 decimal places, use the formula to solve the equation:

$$x = \frac{3 \pm \sqrt{(-3)^2 - 4 \times 10 \times -11}}{2 \times 10}$$

$$= \frac{3 \pm \sqrt{449}}{20}$$

$$= 1.21, -0.91$$

Substitute in $y = \dfrac{3x - 7}{4}$ to find the y-values.

$$y = -0.84, -2.43$$

Exercise 3.17

1 Solve the following simultaneous equations:

  $x + 3y = 2$

  $x^2 + 2y - 3y^2 = 48$

2 Solve the following simultaneous equations, giving your answers to 2 decimal places:

  $2x + 3y = 5$

  $2x - 3y^2 - 2x^2 = -5$

Answers 3.17

1 $x = 2 - 3y$

  $(2 - 3y)^2 + 2y - 3y^2 = 48$

  $4 - 12y + 9y^2 + 2y - 3y^2 = 48$

  $6y^2 - 10y - 44 = 0$

  $3y^2 - 5y - 22 = 0$

  $(3y - 11)(y + 2) = 0$

  $y = \dfrac{11}{3}, -2$

  $x = -9, 8$

2 Make y the subject as it only appears once in the quadratic equation:

  $y = \dfrac{5 - 2x}{3}$

  $2x - 3\left(\dfrac{5 - 2x}{3}\right)^2 - 2x^2 = -5$

  Remember to square the denominator, 3, as well as the numerator:

  $2x - \dfrac{3(25 - 20x + 4x^2)}{9} - 2x^2 = -5$

  $2x - \dfrac{(25 - 20x + 4x^2)}{3} - 2x^2 = -5$

  $6x - (25 - 20x + 4x^2) - 6x^2 = -15$

  $6x - 25 + 20x - 4x^2 - 6x^2 = -15$

  $10x^2 - 26x + 10 = 0$

  $5x^2 - 13x + 5 = 0$

  giving $x = 2.13, 0.47$

  $y = 0.25, 1.35$

TAKE A BREAK

This is a good time for another break.

Linear inequalities

● means including

○ means not including

$-2 \leqslant x < 5$ means x is between -2 and 5, includes -2 but not 5.

On a number line:

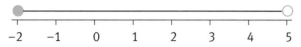

Inequalities are very similar to equations, but with two important differences.

1 If you swap the entire left and right-hand sides, then the inequality reverses.

2 If you multiply or divide by a negative number, then the inequality sign is reversed.

Example 3.39

Find the range of values of x for which $3 - 2x < 7$

Solution

Method 1: taking the $2x$ over to make the coefficient positive

$3 < 2x + 7$

$2x + 7 > 3$ Swapping the sides and reversing the inequality (Rule 1).

$2x > -4$

$x > -2$

Method 2: dividing by -2

$3 - 2x < 7$

$-2x < 4$

$x > -2$ The inequality reverses when dividing by a negative number (Rule 2).

You are probably less likely to make a mistake by using Method 1.

Example 3.40

Find the largest integer for which $7x + 1 < 46$

Solution

Solving the inequality gives $x < 6.43$

The largest integer that satisfies this inequality is 6.

Example 3.41

Find the range of values of x for which

$2x + 5 < 3x + 7 \leqslant 2x + 16$

Solution

Solving $2x + 5 < 3x + 7$ gives $x > -2$ or $-2 < x$

Solving $3x + 7 \leqslant 2x + 16$ gives $x \leqslant 9$

To satisfy both inequalities the range is $-2 < x \leqslant 9$

Exercise 3.18

Find the range of values of x which satisfy the following inequalities.

1   $5 - 4x \leqslant 11$

2   $2 - 7x > 10 - 9x$

3   $x + 4 < 9 + 3x$

4   $x - 2 \leqslant 4x + 1 < 2x + 7$

Answers 3.18

1   $x \geqslant -1.5$ 2 $x > 4$ 3 $x > -2.5$ 4 $-1 \leqslant x < 3$

Inequalities involving x^2

Remember $B \leqslant TW \leqslant \leqslant N$ for $x^2 \leqslant$ or $x^2 <$ questions, and $\leqslant \geqslant UTSII \geqslant E$ for $x^2 \geqslant$ and $x^2 >$ questions.

Example 3.42

Find the range of values of x for which:

a) $x^2 \leqslant 4$

b) $x^2 > 4$

Solution

a)   From the graph, the $y = x^2$ curve is below (i.e. less than) the $y = 4$ line when x is $B \leqslant TW \leqslant \leqslant N$ -2 and 2.

    $-2 \leqslant x \leqslant 2$

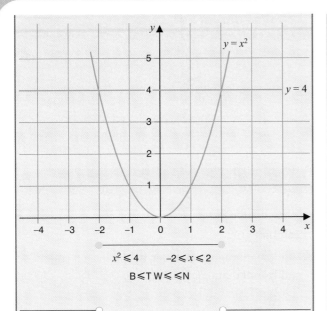

$$x^2 \leqslant 4 \qquad -2 \leqslant x \leqslant 2$$

BETWEEN

$$x^2 > 4$$

OUTSIDE

$$x < -2 \qquad x > 2$$

b) From the graph, $y = x^2$ is above $y = 4$ OUTSIDE -2 and 2. Therefore $x < -2$ and $x > 2$

These must be written as two separate inequalities as the regions are different.

Exercise 3.19

Find the range of values of x which satisfy these inequalities.

1 $x^2 \geqslant 25$ **2** $x^2 < 9$

3 $2x^2 \geqslant 32$ **4** $x^2 + 3 \leqslant 39$

Answers 3.19

4 $-6 \leqslant x \leqslant 6$ **3** $x \geqslant 4, x \leqslant -4$

2 $-3 < x < 3$ **1** $x \geqslant 5, x \leqslant -5$

Algebraic fractions

When cancelling fractions, only cross out terms that appear in both denominator and numerator if all the terms are multiplied.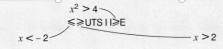

For example, you can cancel out x in $\dfrac{px}{qx}$ to make $\dfrac{p}{q}$.

What you are doing is dividing the top and bottom of the algebraic fractions by x.

However, you cannot cancel x in $\dfrac{p+x}{q+x}$, because you cannot divide top and bottom through by x.

Example 3.43

Simplify the following fractions, where possible.

a) $\dfrac{xy}{x^2}$ **b)** $\dfrac{pqr}{qr^2}$

c) $\dfrac{ab + d}{ab + c}$ **d)** $\dfrac{x^2 + 1}{x^2 + x}$

e) $\dfrac{(x + 1)(x - 2)}{(x - 3)(x + 1)}$

Solution

a) As both the numerator and denominator are divisible by x, you can cancel x in both.

$$\frac{xy}{x^2} = \frac{y}{x}$$

b) As both numerator and denominator are divisible by q and r, the fraction can be simplified.

$$\frac{pqr}{qr^2} = \frac{p}{r}$$

c) This fraction cannot be simplified because the numerator and denominator have no common factors.

You cannot divide by ab.

d) This cannot be simplified because the numerator and denominator have no common factors.

You cannot divide by x^2.

e) As the terms in the numerator and the denominator contain the common factor $(x + 1)$, you can cancel them. (Really you are dividing top and bottom through by $(x + 1)$.)

$$\frac{(x + 1)(x - 2)}{(x - 3)(x + 1)} = \frac{(x - 2)}{(x - 3)}$$

Exercise 3.20

Simplify the following, where possible.

a) $\dfrac{xy}{x^2 z}$ **b)** $\dfrac{pq + r}{qr^2 + p}$

c) $\dfrac{ab^2}{bc}$ **d)** $\dfrac{y^2 + z}{y^2 + x}$

e) $\dfrac{(x + 2)(x - 3)}{(x - 1)(x + 2)}$

Answers 3.20

e) $\dfrac{(x - 3)}{(x - 1)}$

c) $\dfrac{ab}{c}$ **d)** Cannot be simplified

a) $\dfrac{y}{xz}$ **b)** Cannot be simplified

Simplifying more complicated algebraic fractions

Always try to factorise the numerator and denominator of algebraic fractions, then simplify.

Exercise 3.21

Simplify the following:

a) $\dfrac{x^2 + x}{2x + 2}$

b) $\dfrac{3y + 9}{y^2 - 9}$

c) $\dfrac{x^2 - x - 12}{4x - 16}$

d) $\dfrac{x^2 + 10x + 21}{x^2 + 2x - 35}$

e) $\dfrac{2x^2 - 7x + 3}{4x^2 - 1}$

Answers 3.21

e) $\dfrac{2x^2 - 7x + 3}{4x^2 - 1} = \dfrac{(2x - 1)(x - 3)}{(2x - 1)(2x + 1)} = \dfrac{x - 3}{2x + 1}$

d) $\dfrac{x^2 + 10x + 21}{x^2 + 2x - 35} = \dfrac{(x + 7)(x + 3)}{(x + 7)(x - 5)} = \dfrac{x + 3}{x - 5}$

c) $\dfrac{x^2 - x - 12}{4x - 16} = \dfrac{(x - 4)(x + 3)}{4(x - 4)} = \dfrac{x + 3}{4}$

b) $\dfrac{3y + 9}{y^2 - 9} = \dfrac{3(y + 3)}{(y - 3)(y + 3)} = \dfrac{3}{y - 3}$

a) $\dfrac{x^2 + x}{2x + 2} = \dfrac{x(x + 1)}{2(x + 1)} = \dfrac{x}{2}$

Adding and subtracting algebraic fractions

Think back to addition and subtraction of fractions,
e.g. $\dfrac{2}{3} - \dfrac{1}{4}$

The lowest common denominator (LCD) of 3 and 4 is 12:

$\dfrac{2}{3} \times \dfrac{4}{4} = \dfrac{8}{12}$ $\dfrac{1}{4} \times \dfrac{3}{3} = \dfrac{3}{12}$ so $\dfrac{2}{3} - \dfrac{1}{4} = \dfrac{8 - 3}{12} = \dfrac{5}{12}$

Example 3.44

Simplify $\dfrac{3}{x - 4} - \dfrac{1}{x - 1}$

Solution

The LCD is $(x - 4)(x - 1)$

$\dfrac{3}{x - 4} - \dfrac{1}{x - 1} = \dfrac{3(x - 1)}{(x - 4)(x - 1)} - \dfrac{(x - 4)}{(x - 4)(x - 1)}$

Don't forget the brackets around the $(x - 4)$

$= \dfrac{3(x - 1) - (x - 4)}{(x - 4)(x - 1)} = \dfrac{3x - 3 - x + 4}{(x - 4)(x - 1)} = \dfrac{2x + 1}{(x - 4)(x - 1)}$

Exercise 3.22

Simplify:

a) $\dfrac{4}{x - 2} + \dfrac{2}{x + 1}$

b) $\dfrac{2}{x - 3} - \dfrac{1}{3x - 2}$

c) $\dfrac{4x - 3}{6} - \dfrac{2x - 1}{3}$

Answers 3.22

c) $\dfrac{9}{4x - 3 - 2(2x - 1)} = \dfrac{9}{-1}$

b) $\dfrac{2(3x - 2) - 1(x - 3)}{(x - 3)(3x - 2)} = \dfrac{5x - 1}{(x - 3)(3x - 2)}$

a) $\dfrac{4(x + 1) + 2(x - 2)}{(x - 2)(x + 1)} = \dfrac{6x}{(x - 2)(x + 1)}$

Example 3.45

Solve the equation $\dfrac{2x + 1}{6} - \dfrac{3x - 4}{5} = 2$

Solution

Multiply through both sides by the lowest common multiple of 6 and 5, i.e. 30.

$\dfrac{30(2x + 1)}{6} - \dfrac{30(3x - 4)}{5} = 30 \times 2$

$5(2x + 1) - 6(3x - 4) = 60$

$-8x + 29 = 60$

$x = -3\dfrac{7}{8}$

Solving algebraic equations

Multiply both sides of the equation through by the lowest common denominator.

If the question had been given as:

a) Write the following algebraic expression as a single fraction:

$\dfrac{2x + 1}{6} - \dfrac{3x - 4}{5}$

b) Solve $\dfrac{2x + 1}{6} - \dfrac{3x - 4}{5} = 2$

then the solution to part a) would be $\dfrac{-8x + 29}{30}$

so part b) would be $\dfrac{-8x + 29}{30} = 2$

Just multiply both sides by 30: $-8x + 29 = 60$

then proceed as with the given example.

Example 3.46

a) Simplify $\dfrac{3}{2x - 1} - \dfrac{2}{x + 4}$

b) Solve $\dfrac{3}{2x - 1} - \dfrac{2}{x + 4} = 5$, giving your answers to 2 decimal places.

Solution

a) $\dfrac{3(x + 4) - 2(2x - 1)}{(2x - 1)(x + 4)} = \dfrac{14 - x}{(2x - 1)(x + 4)}$

b) $14 - x = 5(2x - 1)(x + 4)$

$10x^2 + 36x - 34 = 0$

$5x^2 + 18x - 17 = 0$

$x = 0.78, -4.38$

Exercise 3.23

1 Solve $\dfrac{3x-2}{3} - \dfrac{5x+1}{2} = 2$

2 Solve $\dfrac{11-x}{4} = \dfrac{5+3x}{6} + 2$

Answers 3.23

1 Multiply through by 6:

$2(3x-2) - 3(5x+1) = 12$

$-9x - 7 = 12$

$x = -\dfrac{19}{9}$ or $-2\frac{1}{9}$

2 Multiply both sides by the lowest common multiple of 4 and 6, i.e. 12

$3(11-x) = 2(5+3x) + 24$

$33 - 3x = 34 + 6x$

$9x = -1$

$x = -\dfrac{1}{9}$

 TAKE A BREAK

You've worked really hard to get through the chapter so far. You're almost there!

Equations in real life

Example 3.47

A rectangular grille is made up of six horizontal bars, each of length x cm, and two vertical bars. The total length of the bars is 72 cm and the area of the grille is 96 cm^2.

a) Show that x satisfies the quadratic equation $x^2 - 12x + 32 = 0$

b) Solve the equation to find the possible widths and heights of the grille.

Solution

a) Let y stand for the height of the grille.

There are six horizontal bars (total length $6x$) and two vertical bars (total length $2y$). Form an equation in x and y.

$6x + 2y = 72$ **1**

The area of the grille is 96 cm^2.

Form an equation in x and y.

$xy = 96$ **2**

The easiest way to solve these simultaneous equations is by substitution. Use equation **1** to write y in terms of x.

$6x + 2y = 72$

$2y = 72 - 6x$

$y = 36 - 3x$

Substitute into equation **2**.

$x(36 - 3x) = 96$

$36x - 3x^2 = 96$

$3x^2 - 36x + 96 = 0$

Divide through by 3.

$x^2 - 12x + 32 = 0$

b) $x^2 - 12x + 32 = 0$

$(x - 4)(x - 8) = 0$

So $x = 4$ cm or $x = 8$ cm.

Substitute into equation **1** to find the solutions.

When $x = 4$, $y = 24$ and when $x = 8$, $y = 12$.

Even if you could not do the first part of the question, you can still try the second part. Always look at the whole question, as you may be able to do the later parts even if you can't do the first part. **Hints & Tips**

Example 3.48

Amy cycles 56 km. Her speed for the first 32 km is x km/h, but for the remaining 24 km it falls to $(x - 2)$ km/h. The journey takes 8 hours.

a) Show that the value of x satisfies the equation $x^2 - 9x + 8 = 0$

b) Solve the equation to find the value of x.

Solution

a) Set up an equation to connect the times taken on the two parts of her trip.

The time for the first 32 km is $\dfrac{32}{x}$ hours.

The time taken for the last 24 km is $\dfrac{24}{x-2}$ hours.

The total time taken is 8 hours.

$$\frac{32}{x} + \frac{24}{x-2} = 8$$

Multiply the whole equation by $x(x-2)$.

$$\frac{32}{x} \times x(x-2) + \frac{24}{x-2} \times x(x-2) = 8 \times x(x-2)$$

$$32(x-2) + 24x = 8x(x-2)$$

$$32x - 64 + 24x = 8x^2 - 16x$$

$$8x^2 - 72x + 64 = 0$$

$$x^2 - 9x + 8 = 0$$

b) $x^2 - 9x + 8 = 0$

$(x-1)(x-8) = 0$

If $x = 1$, then $x - 2 = -1$, a negative speed. This answer is not sensible.

The solution is $x = 8$

Exercise 3.24

1 A rectangular lawn has dimensions $7\,\text{m} \times 6\,\text{m}$. A path of width x metres is laid around the lawn so that the path and lawn form a larger rectangle.

    a) Show that the area of the path is $4x^2 + 26x$ metres.

    b) If the area of the path is 20 metres, find x to 1 decimal place.

2 A man cycles to work, a distance of 18 kilometres, at an average speed of x km/h. When he cycles home from work, he cycles at $(x - 2)$ km/h. If he spends a total of 2 hours cycling to and from work, find an equation in x and hence find x.

Answers 3.24

1 a) Area of path $= (2x + 7)(2x + 6) - 7 \times 6$

    $= 4x^2 + 14x + 12x + 42 - 42$

    $= 4x^2 + 26x$

b) $4x^2 + 26x = 20$

    $2x^2 + 13x - 10 = 0$

    $x = 0.7$ (the negative solution is not possible)

---

2 $\dfrac{18}{x} + \dfrac{18}{x-2} = 2$

Multiplying through by $x(x-2)$ gives

$18(x-2) + 18x = 2x(x-2)$

$36x - 36 = 2x^2 - 4x$

$2x^2 - 40x + 36 = 0$

$x^2 - 20x + 18 = 0$

$x = 19.1$ or 0.9

So $x = 19.1$ (the other solution makes $x - 2$ a negative number).

Sequences

When you are working with sequences, you should note first of all whether the spacings are equal (e.g. 2, 4, 6, 8 …) or whether the spacings get larger (e.g. 1, 3, 6, 10, …).

*Then you can use **DINO** or **COSTAS** to help.*

***DINO** is used to find the nth term of an equally spaced sequence.*

***DI** stands for the difference (it is negative if the numbers are decreasing).*

***N** stands for the variable (usually n).*

***O** stands for the term before the first (i.e. the 0th term).*

***COSTAS** is to help with unequally spaced sequences. It stands for **C**ube **O**r **S**quare, **T**imes, **A**dd, **S**ubtract.*

Sequences with equal spacing

Example 3.49

Look at the sequence 9, 16, 23, 30, …

a) What is the difference between consecutive terms?

b) What is the next term in the sequence?

c) What is the nth term?

d) What is the 25th term?

Solution

a) The difference between consecutive terms
$= 30 - 23 = 23 - 16 = 16 - 9 = 7$

b) The next term is $30 + 7 = 37$

c) Here we can use DINO, as the numbers are evenly spaced, with a difference of 7. Put a ring before the first term.

$\bigcirc$ 9, 16, 23, 30, …

What number would go in here if there were a number before the 9?

$9 - 7 = 2$

② 9, 16, 23, 30, …

DI stands for the difference (7), N stands for n and O stands for the number in the ring (2).

DINO gives $7n + 2$.

Check: If you put $n = 1$, you should get the first term, $7 \times 1 + 2 = 9$; $n = 2$ gives the second term, 16, etc.

The nth term is $7n + 2$.

d) What is the 25th term?

Put $n = 25$, which gives $7 \times 25 + 2 = 177$

Questions often ask for the nth term after they ask for the 25th term, but it is easier to use DINO first then substitute $n = 25$ to find the 25th term.

If you are asked to find n for a given term, find the formula using DINO and then equate it to the given value.

Equally spaced sequences with negative differences

Example 3.50

Look at the sequence 10, 7, 4, 1, ...

a) Find the next two terms.

b) Find the nth term.

c) Find the 50th term.

d) If the value of the kth term is −83, find k.

Solution

a) Since the values of the terms are decreasing, the difference is negative.
The difference is −3, so the next two terms are −2, −5.

b) Using DINO, DI = −3 N = n O = 13
(adding 3 to 10).
So the nth term is $-3n + 13$.

c) The 50th term = $-3 \times 50 + 13 = -137$

d) Substituting the values for the kth term:
$$-3k + 13 = -83$$
$$96 = 3k$$
$$k = 32$$

Fractions made from sequences with equal spacing

Sequences that involve fractions are often made up of two separate sequences, one forming the numerators and the other forming the denominators.

Example 3.51

Look at the sequence $\frac{3}{4}, \frac{5}{7}, \frac{7}{10}, \frac{9}{13}, \dots$

a) Write down the next two terms.

b) Find the nth term.

c) Find the 12th term.

Solution

a) The values of the numerators of the terms are increasing by 2 each time. The values of the denominators are increasing by 3 each time.
The next two terms are: $\frac{11}{16}, \frac{13}{19}$.

b) The sequence in the numerators is given by $2n + 1$.
The sequence in the denominators is given by $3n + 1$.
The nth term is $\dfrac{2n + 1}{3n + 1}$

c) The 12th term is $\dfrac{2 \times 12 + 1}{3 \times 12 + 1} = \dfrac{25}{37}$

If your sequence is given as a series of fractions, look at the spacings in the numerators and in the denominators. Treat them as two different sequences.

Exercise 3.25

For each of these sequences:

i) Write down the next two terms.

ii) Find the nth term.

iii) Find the 40th term.

a) 1, 4, 7, 10, ...

b) 10, 8, 6, 4, ...

c) $1, 1\frac{1}{3}, 1\frac{2}{3}, 2, \dots$

d) $\frac{2}{3}, \frac{5}{7}, \frac{8}{11}, \frac{11}{15}, \dots$

Answers 3.25

a) (i) 13, 16 (ii) $3n - 2$ (iii) 118

b) (i) 2, 0 (ii) $-2n + 12$ (iii) −68

c) (i) $2\frac{1}{3}, 2\frac{2}{3}$ (ii) $\frac{1}{3}n + \frac{2}{3}$ (iii) 14

d) (i) $\frac{14}{17}, \frac{17}{23}$ (ii) $\dfrac{3n - 1}{4n - 1}$ (iii) $\dfrac{119}{159}$

Unequally spaced sequences

Example 3.52

The following numbers form a sequence.

3, 6, 11, 18, ...

a) What is the next term in the sequence?

b) What is the nth term in the sequence?

Solution

a) Look at the differences between the terms.

3, 5, 7, ...

It can be seen that the difference increases by 2 every term, so the next difference must be 9. The next term must be $18 + 9 = 27$.

3, 6, 11, 18, 27

b) COSTAS may be used as the differences are not equal.

COSTAS stands for

Cube Or Square, Times, Add, Subtract.

Write the sequence down, with the number of each term above it.

n	1	2	3	4
nth term	3	6	11	18

First try squaring the n (as squaring is easier than cubing), and comparing to see if you can see a link between the squared numbers and each term. (If you can't, then you can try cubing them.)

n	1	2	3	4
n^2	1	4	9	16
nth term	3	6	11	18

You can see that you have to add 2 to n^2 to get the term. So the nth term is $n^2 + 2$

Example 3.53

Find the nth term of the sequence
2, 6, 12, 20, 30, ...

Solution

An alternative method is to write down a row of differences, then differences between the differences, etc. until all the numbers in the row are equal:

```
  2    6    12    20    30
     4    6     8     10
        2    2     2
```

As the second row of differences are equal, the sequence involves n^2. If it were the third row, it would be a cubic sequence.

n	1	2	3	4	5
n^2	1	4	9	16	25
	2	6	12	20	30

From TAS of COSTAS, the sequence is $n^2 + n$

Alternative method for finding quadratic or cubic sequences

As the second row of differences are equal, the sequence is quadratic and of the form $an^2 + bn + c$ Substitute when $n = 1$, term = 2; when $n = 2$, term = 6; when $n = 3$, term = 12 into the quadratic and solve using simultaneous equations:

$n = 3$:	$9a + 3b + c = 12$	(3)
$n = 2$:	$4a + 2b + c = 6$	(2)
$n = 1$:	$a + b + c = 2$	(1)
(3) − (2)	$5a + b = 6$	(4)
(2) − (1)	$3a + b = 4$	(5)
(4) − (5)	$2a = 2$	
	$a = 1$	

Substituting into (5) gives $b = 1$

Substituting into (3) gives $c = 0$

So the sequence is $n^2 + n$

If the sequence is cubic, the nth term of the sequence is of the form $an^3 + bn^3 + cn + d$

Example 3.54

Find an expression for the nth term in the following sequence.

2, 16, 54, 128, ...

Solution

Write the numbers 1, 2, 3, 4 above the corresponding terms, leaving a space in between.

n	1	2	3	4
	2	16	54	128

Using COSTAS, start by squaring n.

n	1	2	3	4
n^2	1	4	9	16
	2	16	54	128

Comparing the n^2 line with the bottom line and using the TAS of COSTAS (which stands for Times, Add, Subtract), there is no way of finding a link between the numbers in the two lines. You don't need the n^2 line, so put a line through it.

We've used the first S from COSTAS, so now we try the C (cube).

n	1	2	3	4
~~n^2~~	~~1~~	~~4~~	~~9~~	~~16~~
n^3	1	8	27	64
	2	16	54	128

Using the TAS of COSTAS, you can clearly see that to find the bottom line you multiply the numbers in the n^3 row by 2.

So the nth term is $2 \times n^3$, or $2n^3$

The 3–5–7 sequence (a quicker method for some unequally spaced sequences)

This works for sequences which have differences between terms of 3, then 5, then 7, etc.

n^2 is the sequence 1, 4, 9, 16, … and the differences are 3, 5, 7, 9, …, so all the following sequences are based upon adding a number to this.

Example 3.55

Find the nth term of the sequence 10, 13, 18, 25, …

Solution

The differences in the sequence are 3, 5, 7, …

Subtracting 1 from the first term gives 9, so the nth term of the sequence is:

$n^2 + 9$

Example 3.56

Find an expression for the nth term of the sequence 5, 8, 13, 20, …

Solution

The nth term is $n^2 + 4$. Check it for yourself.

Fibonacci sequences

These are sequences in which each term is the sum of the two previous terms.

Example 3.57

Find the next three terms in the sequence 1, 1, 2, 3, 5, 8, …

Solution

Using the rule, the next three terms are
8 + 5 = 13, 13 + 8 = 21, 21 + 13 = 34

Triangular numbers

Example 3.58

The sequence of triangular numbers is 1, 3, 6, 10, …
a) Write down the formula for the nth term.
b) Write down and simplify the formula for the nth term of the sequence 100, 300, 600, 1000.

Solution

a) The differences are a sequence 2, 3, 4, …
The formula for the nth term is $\frac{1}{2}n(n + 1)$

b) Each term in this sequence is 100 times the corresponding term in the triangular numbers. The formula for the nth term is $100 \times \frac{1}{2}n(n + 1)$ or $50n(n + 1)$

Exercise 3.26

1 In the sequence 1, 4, 7, 10, 13, …
   a) find the 16th term
   b) find which term gives the number 139
   c) give a formula for the nth term.

2 For the sequence 8, 11, 16, 23, 32, … , find:
   a) the 14th term   b) the nth term.

3 For the sequence 5, 12, 19, 26, … find:
   a) the 25th term   b) the nth term.

4 Find the nth term of the sequence 3, 12, 27, 48, …

5 Find the next two terms in the sequence 2, 4, 6, 10, 16, …

6 Find the nth term in the sequence 4, 11, 30, 67, …

Answers 3.26

1 a) 46 b) 47 c) $3n - 2$
2 a) 203 b) $n^2 + 7$
3 a) 173 b) $7n - 2$
4 $3n^2$ 5 … 26, 42 6 $n^3 + 3$

Proofs

If you are given a statement to prove, write one of the numbers as x, or in terms of x. For example, if the number is described as a square number, call it x^2. Then write the statement as an expression in x, and solve or simplify as required.

Example 3.59

Prove that the sum of three consecutive numbers is always divisible by three.

Solution

In this type of question it is not enough to provide examples showing that the rule works (e.g. 7 + 8 + 9 = 24; this is a multiple of 3). As we cannot add together all the numbers that exist, we need to make a general formula.

Choose a letter to represent the first number: x
The next consecutive number is $x + 1$
The third number is $x + 2$
The sum of the three numbers is
$x + x + 1 + x + 2 = 3x + 3$
Factorising this gives $3(x + 1)$, so the number is divisible by 3.

Exercise 3.27

Prove that the difference between two consecutive square numbers is always an odd number.

Answers 3.27

Let the first number be x^2. The next number is

$(x + 1)^2 = x^2 + 2x + 1$

The difference is $x^2 + 2x + 1 - x^2 = 2x + 1$

$2x$ is always even, so $2x + 1$ is always odd.

 **TAKE A BREAK**

So you think you've got it?

Exam-type questions 3

1 Here are the first five terms of a number sequence. 2, 8, 14, 20, 26
   a) Give a rule for the next term.
   b) Find the value of the 22nd term.
   c) Find an expression for the nth term.

2 Expand the following expressions.
   a) $(x - 1)(x + 6)$ b) $(6x + 1) - (x - 1)$
   c) $(c - d)(c + d)$ d) $(2x - 3)^2$

3 a) Rearrange the formula $V = \frac{4}{3}\pi r^3$ to give r in terms of V and π.
   b) Find the value of r when $V = 2017$.

4 Five pens and three rubbers cost 192 pence. Seven pens and six rubbers cost 303 pence.

   a) Write this information as two equations using x to represent the cost in pence of a pen, and y to represent the cost in pence of a rubber.
   b) Solve the equations to find x and y.

5 Factorise the following expressions.
   a) $8a^2b - 12ab^2$ b) $10b^2c^2 + 5bc$
   c) $x^2 - x - 6$ d) $2x^2 - 13x + 15$

6 a) Show that $x^{-1} = 3(x + 2)$ can be written as $3x^2 + 6x - 1 = 0$
   b) Find the roots of this equation correct to 2 d.p.

7 Solve the following inequalities for x.
   a) $x^2 < 1$ b) $3x^2 > 12$ c) $x + 6 < 4x - 15$

8 The next term in the sequence
   1, 1, 6, 21, ...
   can be found by adding the previous two terms and multiplying the result by 3. Give the next two numbers in the sequence.

9 a) Factorise the expression $x^2 + x - 12$
   b) Hence or otherwise solve the equation $x^2 + x = 12$

10 Find the values of x and y in the following pairs of equations.
   a) $5x + 4y = 10$ b) $2x - 3y = 10$
      $y = x + 7$ $3x - 5y = 21$

11 a) Factorise the expression $a^2 - b^2$
   b) Using the information from a), and without a calculator, evaluate $52^2 - 49^2$. Show your working.

12 Use trial and improvement to find a value for x correct to 2 d.p. which satisfies the equation $x^3 - 2x = 95$. Start with the value $x = 5$.

13 Rearrange the following formulae to give x in terms of y and z.
   a) $y = \dfrac{z}{x + 1}$ b) $y = \dfrac{\pi\sqrt{x}}{z}$ c) $x^3 + 4 = yz$

REVIEW

How much have you learnt?
Tick off each topic in the list when you are
confident that you can cope with it.

- ☐ Factorise simple algebraic expressions.
- ☐ Rearrange formulae.
- ☐ Solve simultaneous equations algebraically.
- ☐ Solve equations using trial and improvement.
- ☐ Multiply out brackets.
- ☐ Factorise quadratic expressions.
- ☐ Solve quadratic equations.
- ☐ Complete the square.
- ☐ Solve simultaneous equations with a linear and a quadratic expression.
- ☐ Solve inequalities.
- ☐ Simplify and manipulate algebraic fractions.
- ☐ Solve equations from real-life situations.
- ☐ Find the nth terms of sequences.
- ☐ Find the next terms in Fibonacci sequences.
- ☐ Prove statements using algebra.

PREVIEW

By the end of this chapter you will be able to:

- **identify the gradient and *y*-intercept from the equation of a straight line**
- **distance between and midpoint of two points**
- **solve simultaneous equations graphically**
- **sketch graphs of quadratic equations**
- **convert a non-linear graph to a linear graph by changing variables**
- **find values of the constants in a non-linear function**
- **transform functions**
- **draw trigonometric graphs**
- **find the values of an unknown, in a given range, that satisfy a trigonometric equation**
- **find a range of values that satisfy an algebraic inequality**
- **maximise or minimise an expression**
- **recognise graphs of mathematical equations**
- **find a graphical region which satisfies inequalities.**

Straight-line graphs

Straight-line graphs have equations or formulae of the form:

$$y = mx + c \quad \text{or} \quad ax + by = c$$

Gradient and *y*-intercept

There are two alternative ways of tackling questions involving straight-line graphs. You may need either approach.

1 – The algebraic method

If your equation is not in the form $y = mx + c$, then rearrange it so that it is.

m gives the gradient   *c* gives the *y*-intercept

For example, if the equation is $y = 2x - 1$, the gradient = 2, the *y*-intercept = -1.

If the equation is $2y + x = 2$, rearrange it to make *y* the subject of the formula.

$$2y = 2 - x$$

Halving all terms gives:

$$y = 1 - \tfrac{1}{2}x \quad \text{or} \quad y = -\tfrac{1}{2}x + 1$$

gradient = $-\tfrac{1}{2}$

y-intercept = 1

2 – Tabulation

Draw up a table inserting sensible values for *x*. Sometimes you may be able to use a short cut, especially for equations of the form $ax + by = c$.

For example, if the equation is $2x + 5y = 20$, substitute $x = 0$ to give $y = 4$, and substitute $y = 0$ to give $x = 10$.

Plot the points (0, 4) and (10, 0) and join them up.

It is always wise to check by finding a third point and making sure it is on the line you have drawn.

Example 4.1

Find the gradient of the line.

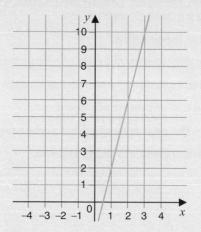

Solution

Choose two points on the line and draw a right-angled triangle. Use it to work out the gradient, remembering
Gradients are GROTty
(Gradient = Rise Over Tread) or
Gradients are GRADUAL (GRADient = Up/ALong)
or your own method.

From the diagram: gradient = $\dfrac{8}{2} = 4$

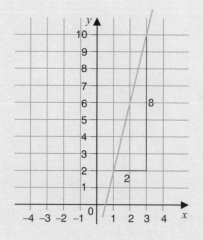

Linear graphs and $y = mx + c$

Most straight-line (linear) graphs can be written in the form $y = mx + c$, where m is the gradient and c is the value of the y-intercept.

If y is not the subject of the formula, rearrange the equation before using this method.

Example 4.2

Write down the gradient and the y-intercept of the following graphs.

a) $y = 4x - 1$

b) $y = 1 - x$

c) $4x + 3y = 24$

Solution

a) Gradient = 4, y-intercept = −1.

b) This equation may be rewritten as $y = -x + 1$, so the gradient = −1 (the coefficient of x), and the y-intercept = 1

c) $3y = 24 - 4x \Rightarrow y = 8 - \dfrac{4x}{3}$

Gradient = $-\dfrac{4}{3}$, y-intercept = 8

Example 4.3

Find the equation of the line which passes through the points (4, 3) and (6, −5).

Solution

Gradient = $\dfrac{\text{change in } y}{\text{change in } x} = \dfrac{-5 - 3}{6 - 4} = -4$

If you are having difficulty with the sign of the gradient, try using the formula $\dfrac{y_2 - y_1}{x_2 - x_1}$

So the equation of the graph is of the form $y = -4x + c$

Substitute either of the pairs of coordinates into this equation to find c.

$\quad$ Using (4, 3): $3 = -4(4) + c$
$\qquad\qquad\qquad\quad 3 = -16 + c$
$\qquad\qquad\qquad\quad\; c = 19$

So the equation of the line is $y = -4x + 19$

Check that the other point is on this line:
$\quad -5 = -4(6) + 19$

Yes, this is correct.

Example 4.4

a) Find the equation of the line below in the form $y = mx + c$

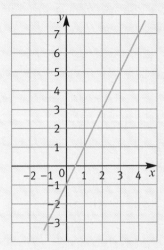

b) Find an equation of a line that is parallel to the graph and passes through the point (0, 3).

Solution

a) Using any two points on the line as the hypotenuse of a right-angled triangle, the gradient = 2. The y-intercept is at −1. So the equation of the line is $y = 2x - 1$

b) If the new line is parallel to the first, it must have the same gradient. The y-intercept is 3. So an equation of the line is $y = 2x + 3$

Drawing linear graphs in the form $y = mx + c$

Draw up a table of values, choosing three values of x (usually 0, 1 and 2 are the easiest). Find the corresponding y-values and plot these coordinates on the grid. If they do not lie in a straight line, you have probably made an error in the calculations or in plotting the points. Connect the points together, extending the graph to the ends of the grid.

Drawing lines of the form $ax + by = c$

Substitute in the value $x = 0$ to find where the line cuts the y-axis, then $y = 0$ to find where it cuts the x-axis. Plot these on the grid, connect them using a ruler and extend this line to the ends of the grid. To check, find another point that your line passes through and verify that the x- and y-values satisfy the equation of the line.

Graphs

The meaning of the gradient

The gradient means the measure on the y-axis divided by that on the x-axis. Alternatively, it means y per x. For example, on a distance-time graph, the gradient gives the speed. On a speed-time graph it gives the acceleration.

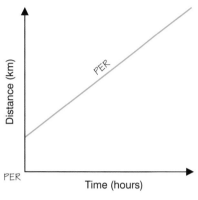

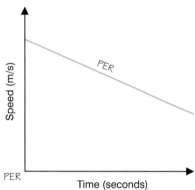

Perpendicular lines

If two lines are perpendicular, the product of their gradients is −1. So to find the gradient of one line you take the reciprocal of the other and change the sign.

Example 4.5

The gradients of a number of lines are given below. Find the gradients of their perpendiculars.

a) $\frac{1}{2}$

b) $-\frac{3}{4}$

c) 4

d) $-\frac{2}{3}$

Solution

Let the gradient of the perpendicular be p.

a) $\frac{1}{2}p = -1$, so $p = -2$

b) $-\frac{3}{4}p = -1$, so $-3p = -4$, so $p = \frac{4}{3}$

c) $4p = -1$, so $p = -\frac{1}{4}$

d) $-\frac{2}{3}p = -1$, so $p = \frac{3}{2}$

Example 4.6

Find an equation of a line perpendicular to the line $5x - 3y = 12$, passing through the point $(5, 4)$.

Solution

Rearranging the given line gives $y = \frac{5}{3}x - 4$

The gradient is therefore $\frac{5}{3}$

The gradient of the perpendicular is $-\frac{3}{5}$

So the perpendicular line is of the form

$y = -\frac{3}{5}x + c$

Now to find c, substitute in $(5, 4)$, putting $x = 5$ and $y = 4$,

$4 = -\frac{3}{5} \times 5 + c$, so $4 = -3 + c$, so $c = 7$

So an equation of the perpendicular is

$y = -\frac{3}{5}x + 7$

This may be written in other ways: if you multiply through by 5:

$5y = -3x + 35$

You can also take the $3x$ over to the left-hand side:

$3x + 5y = 35$

These are all different ways of writing the equation of the same line.

Exercise 4.1

1 Find the gradients of the perpendiculars to the lines given below:

a) $y = 6 - x$

b) $y = 3x - 2$

c) $4x + y = 7$

d) $3x - 7y = 10$

2 Find an equation of the line perpendicular to the line $3x - 2y = 6$, which passes through the point $(9, 2)$.

48

Answers 4.1

1 a) The gradient of the given line is -1, so the perpendicular has gradient 1.

b) The gradient of the given line is 3, so the perpendicular has gradient $-\frac{1}{3}$.

c) Rearranging the equation gives $y = -4x + 7$, so the gradient of the given line is -4. Then the perpendicular has gradient $\frac{1}{4}$.

d) $y = \frac{3}{7}x - \frac{10}{7}$

So the gradient is $\frac{3}{7}$, and the gradient of the perpendicular is $-\frac{7}{3}$

2 Rearranging the equation gives $y = \frac{3}{2}x - 3$, so the gradient of the given line is $\frac{3}{2}$. Then the perpendicular has gradient $-\frac{2}{3}$.

The equation of the perpendicular is of the form

$$y = -\frac{2}{3}x + c$$

Substituting (9, 2) into the equation,

$$2 = -\frac{2}{3} \times 9 + c$$

$$c = 8$$

So $y = -\frac{2}{3}x + 8$

Distance between two points

The method for finding the distance between the two points (x_1, y_1) and (x_2, y_2) is shown in the diagram below.

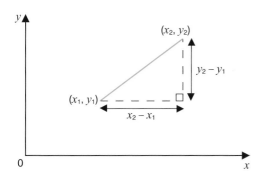

The right-angled triangle has sides of length $(x_2 - x_1)$ and $(y_2 - y_1)$.

By Pythagoras' theorem, the distance between the two points (or the hypotenuse) is

$$\sqrt{(x_2 - x_1)^2 + (y_2 - y_1)^2}$$

Remember *that if the number you are squaring is negative, on most calculators you need to put the negative number in brackets before you square it.*

Example 4.7

Find the distance between the points (4, 5) and (8, 10):

a) leaving your answer as an exact number

b) giving your answer to 1 decimal place.

Solution

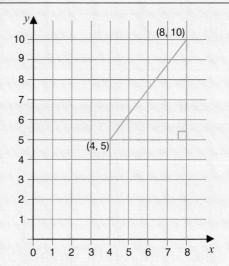

a) $\sqrt{(8-4)^2 + (10-5)^2} = \sqrt{16 + 25} = \sqrt{41}$

b) $\sqrt{41} = 6.4$ correct to 1 d.p.

Finding the midpoint of two points

To find the coordinates of the midpoint of the two points (x_1, y_1) and (x_2, y_2), take the mean of x_1 and x_2, and the mean of y_1 and y_2.

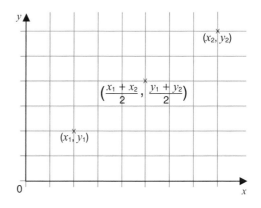

So the midpoint of (x_1, y_1) and (x_2, y_2) is

$$\left(\frac{x_1 + x_2}{2}, \frac{y_1 + y_2}{2} \right)$$

Exercise 4.2

1 Find the distances between the following pairs of points, giving your answers as exact numbers.
 a) (2, 7) and (4, 10)
 b) (−3, 0) and (6, 7)
 c) (−6, −2) and (−1, 5)
2 Find the distances between the following pairs of points, giving your answers to 2 significant figures.
 a) (5, 2) and (6, 9)
 b) (−4, −3) and (6, −8)
 c) (540, 521) and (348, 892)
3 Find the midpoints of the following pairs of points.
 a) (8, 5) and (2, 7)
 b) (−3, −5) and (−9, −1)
 c) (0, 3) and (7, 2)

Answers 4.2

1 a) $\sqrt{13}$ b) $\sqrt{130}$ c) $\sqrt{74}$
2 a) 7.1   b) 11   c) 420
3 a) (5, 6)   b) (−6, −3)   c) (3.5, 2.5)

Solution of quadratic equations

Solving quadratic equations means finding the roots. This can be done by a graphical method.

Sketching graphs of quadratic equations

- Quadratic graphs are symmetrical.
- They have either a minimum or a maximum point.
- They cross the x-axis a maximum of twice.
- Solving a quadratic equation gives the x-values of the points where the curve crosses the x-axis.

Exercise 4.3

Solve the equation $x^2 - 5x + 5 = 0$ graphically.

Answers 4.3

Tabulate the values as follows.

x	−2	−1	0	1	2	3	4	5
$y = x^2 - 5x + 5$	19	11	5	1	−1	−1	1	5

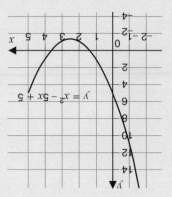

Be careful to join $(2, -1)$ and $(3, -1)$ with a curve.

The curve $y = x^2 - 5x + 5$ crosses the $y = 0$ line (or x-axis) at $x = 1.4$ and $x = 3.6$. These are the roots of the equation $x^2 - 5x + 5 = 0$

Solution of simultaneous equations

Graphical solution

When you are asked to solve simultaneous equations by a graphical method, the equations will be given to you and you need to draw their graphs. The coordinates of the point(s) where they cross (or intersect) will give the solution(s) for x and y.

Example 4.8

Using graph paper, draw accurately the graphs for the following equations.

$x + 2y = 7$ $x - y = 4$

Hence solve these simultaneous equations graphically.

Solution

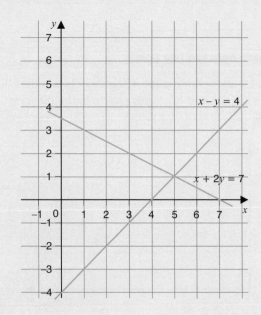

The lines cross at (5, 1), so the solution is $x = 5$, $y = 1$

Solving simultaneous equations involving quadratics graphically

In these questions, you are given a graph and asked to solve an equation by drawing an additional line on it. The key is knowing which line or curve to draw. Take the following steps.

1. Start with the equation that you need to solve.

2. Add or subtract to both sides of the equation to make one side the same as the equation of the graph.

3. Draw the graph of $y =$ 'the other side'.

4. Write down the x-values of the points where the two graphs meet.

Example 4.9

By adding suitable lines to the graph of $y = x^2 + 3x - 2$ (shown below) find the solutions of:

a) $x^2 + 3x - 1 = 0$

b) $x^2 + x - 3 = 0$.

Give your answers correct to 1 decimal place.

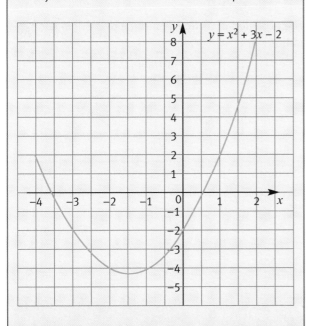

Solution

a) Start by writing $x^2 + 3x - 1 = 0$
-1 from both sides to make the right-hand side the same as $x^2 + 3x - 2$:

$$\frac{x^2 + 3x - 1 = \quad 0}{x^2 + 3x - 2 = -1} \quad \frac{-1 \quad -1}{}$$

So draw the graph of $y = -1$ to the graph, and find the x-values where the graphs cross.
$x = -3.3, 0.3$

b)
$$\frac{x^2 + x - 3 = 0}{x^2 + 3x - 2 = 2x + 1} \quad \frac{+2x+1 \quad +2x+1}{}$$

So draw the graph of $y = 2x + 1$ on the grid and write down the x-values where it crosses the curve.
$x = -2.3, 1.3$

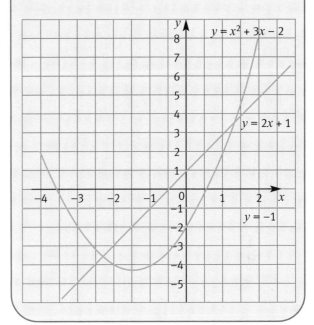

Exercise 4.4

1. The graph of $y = x^2 - x - 3$ is shown below:

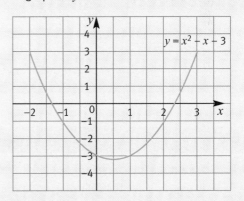

By adding a suitable line to the graph, use the graph to find the solutions of

a) $x^2 - x - 1 = 0$

b) $x^2 - 3x + 1 = 0$

Give your answers to 1 decimal place.

2. If you are given the graph of $y = x^2 - 2x$, what would you draw on the grid to find the solution to these equations?

a) $x^2 - 2x = 4$

b) $x^2 - 4x - 3 = 0$

Answers 4.4

1 a) $x^2 - x - 1 = 0$ **b)** $x^2 - 3x + 1 = 0$

$$
\begin{array}{ll}
x^2 - x - 3 = -2 & x^2 - x - 3 = 2x - 4\\
\underline{\; -2\;\; -2} & \underline{\; +2x-4\;\; +2x-4}
\end{array}
$$

Draw $y = -2$ on the grid.   So draw $y = 2x - 4$.

$x = -0.6, 1.6$ $x = 0.4, 2.6$

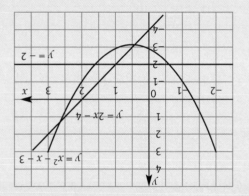

2 a) As the left-hand side of the equation is the same as the equation of the graph, draw the graph of 'y =' the other side'

$y = 4$

b) You need to get $x^2 - 2x$ on one side of this equation. Since the x^2 is on the left-hand side of the equation, make this into $x^2 - 2x$ by adding or subtracting terms to both sides:

$$
\begin{array}{l}
x^2 - 4x - 3 = 0\\
\underline{+2x + 3 \quad +2x + 3}\\
x^2 - 2x = 2x + 3
\end{array}
$$

So $y = 2x + 3$ should be drawn on the grid.

The solutions to part **a)** and **b)** are the x-values of the points where the graphs meet.

Exercise 4.5

By drawing suitable lines on the graph $y = 2x^2 - x$ below, solve the following equations.

a) $2x^2 - x = x + 2$ **b)** $2x^2 - x - 5 = 0$

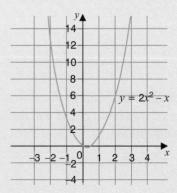

Answers 4.5

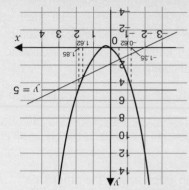

a) Draw $y = x + 2$ on the graph.

The lines cross when $x = 1.6$ and -0.6 so the solution of the equation $2x^2 - x = x + 2$ is $x = 1.6, -0.6$

b) Rearrange the equation so that $2x^2 - x$ is on one side. This gives $2x^2 - x = 5$. Now draw the line $y = 5$.

The lines cross when $x = -1.35$ and 1.85 so the solution is $x = -1.35, 1.85$

Circle graphs

The equation of a circle centred at the origin with radius r is $x^2 + y^2 = r^2$

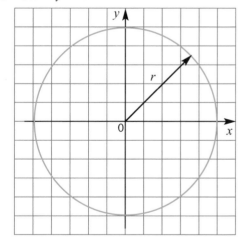

Exercise 4.6

1 What is the radius of a circle with this equation? $x^2 + y^2 = 16$

2 Write down the equation of a circle, centred at the origin with radius 6.

Answers 4.6

1 radius = $\sqrt{16} = 4$

2 $x^2 + y^2 = 36$

Circle graphs and line intersections

Example 4.10

The graph of the circle $x^2 + y^2 = 25$ is given below.

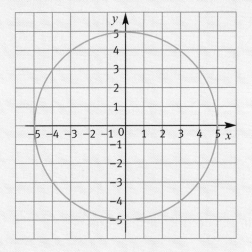

By adding a suitable line to the graph, find the solutions to the given simultaneous equations.

$x^2 + y^2 = 25$

$y = x + 1$

Solution

Add the line $y = x + 1$ to the graph:

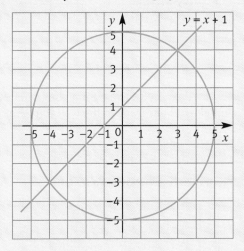

The graphs cross at (3, 4) and (−4, −3).

Exercise 4.7

1 Fully describe the graph drawn by the equation:
$x^2 + y^2 = 100$
2 Draw the graphs of the following equations and find the coordinates of their points of intersection.
$x^2 + y^2 = 64$
$y = x − 2$

Answers 4.7

1 This is a circle, centre (0, 0) and radius 10.
2 The graph of $x^2 + y^2 = 64$ is a circle, centre (0, 0) and radius 8. The straight line graph $y = x − 2$ intersects with the circle at approximately (−4.6, −6.6) and (6.6, 4.6).

TAKE A BREAK

Now is a good time to take a break and think back over what you have done so far.

Finding the values of the constants in a non-linear equation

Example 4.11

Variables y and x are related by the equation $y = ab^x$. The graph below shows the relationship. Using this graph, estimate the values of a and b.

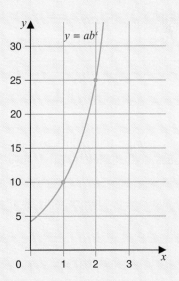

Solution

Substituting $x = 0$ gives $y = ab^0 = a$ (because any number to the power of zero is 1).

So (0, 4) gives the value of a as 4.

When $x = 1$, $y = ab$

As $y = 10$ when $x = 1$, we find $b = 2.5$

The variables x and y are related by the equation $y = ab^x$. If the graph passes through $(0, 3)$ and $(3, 24)$ find the values of a and b.

$(3, 24) \Rightarrow 24 = ab^3 \Rightarrow b^3 = 8 \Rightarrow b = 2$

$(0, 3) \Rightarrow 3 = ab^0 \Rightarrow a = 3$

Functions

A relation between two variables, x and y, can be written as $y = f(x)$.

Adding, subtracting or dividing inside the brackets changes $f(x)$ horizontally in the opposite way to what you would expect:

$y = f(x + c)$ moves $f(x)$ to the **left** by c units,
$y = f(x - c)$ moves $f(x)$ to the **right** by c units.

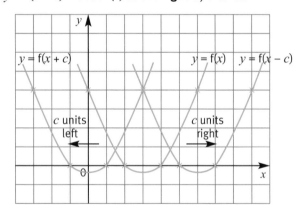

Use crosses at important points so that you draw the solution accurately. Examples are shown on the graphs.

$y = f(2x)$ squashes $f(x)$ horizontally by a factor of 2 towards the y-axis.

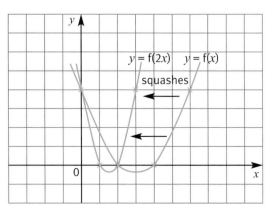

$y = f\left(\dfrac{x}{2}\right)$ or $f\left(\dfrac{1}{2}x\right)$ stretches $f(x)$ horizontally by a factor of 2 from the y-axis.

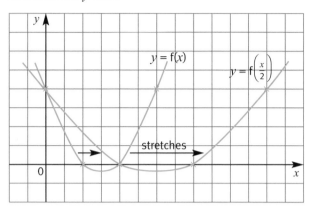

$y = f(-x)$ reflects $f(x)$ in the y-axis.

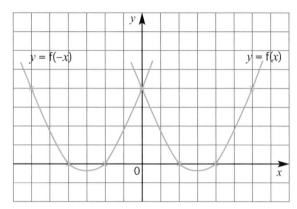

Adding, subtracting, multiplying or dividing outside the $f(x)$ changes $f(x)$ vertically in the way you would expect:

$y = f(x) + c$ moves $f(x)$ **upwards** by c units,

$y = f(x) - c$ moves $f(x)$ **downwards** by c units.

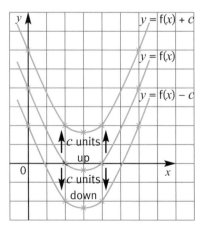

$y = 2f(x)$ **stretches** $f(x)$ vertically by a factor of 2 from the x-axis.

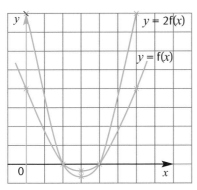

$y = \dfrac{f(x)}{2}$ or $\frac{1}{2}f(x)$ **squashes** $f(x)$ vertically by a factor of 2 towards the x-axis.

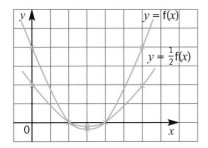

$y = -f(x)$ reflects $f(x)$ in the x-axis.

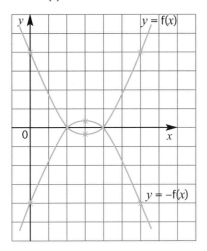

To ensure that your sketch of the new graph is accurate, take a number of points on the graph of $f(x)$ (including turning points and points where the graph crosses the axes) and transform them accordingly. Then sketch the graph. Crosses have been shown on the graphs as suggestions as to where these points may be placed.

Example 4.12

The minimum point of $f(x) = x^2$ is at the origin. Write down the coordinates of the minimum point of:

a) $y = (x + 1)^2$ b) $y = x^2 - 3$

c) $y = (x - 2)^2 - 1$ d) $y = (x + 1)^2 + 4$

Solution

a) This graph is the same as $f(x + 1)$; minimum point is at $(-1, 0)$

b) $y = f(x) - 3$; minimum point is $(0, -3)$

c) $y = f(x - 2) - 1$; minimum point is $(2, -1)$

d) $y = f(x + 1) + 4$; minimum point is $(-1, 4)$

Example 4.13

The graph of $y = x^2$ has been drawn on the grid shown. On the same axes, draw the graphs

a) $y = (x - 2)^2$ b) $y = -x^2$

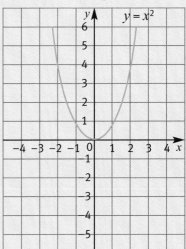

Solution

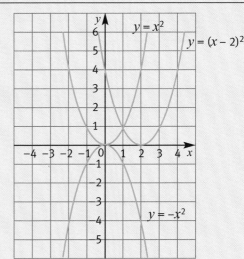

a) $y = (x - 2)^2$ moves the graph of $y = x^2$ by 2 units to the right (if $f(x) = x^2$, then $(x - 2)^2 = f(x - 2)$). Take a number of points on $y = x^2$, and move them 2 units right. Join the points to give the graph of $y = (x - 2)^2$

b) $y = -x^2$ is the reflection of $y = x^2$ in the x-axis. (If $f(x) = x^2$, then $-x^2 = -f(x)$.) Take a few points on $y = x^2$, reflect them in the x-axis, then join them up to give $y = -x^2$

Example 4.14

The graph of $y = \cos x$ is drawn below. On the same grid, draw the graph of $y = 2\cos x$

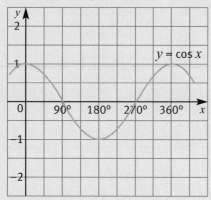

Solution

To find the graph of $y = 2\cos x$ from $y = \cos x$, double the vertical distances of the original graph. (If $f(x) = \cos x$, then $2\cos x = 2f(x)$)

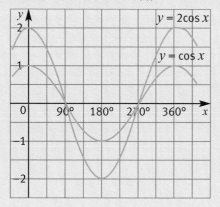

Exercise 4.9

The minimum point of $f(x) = x^2$ is at the origin. Write down the coordinates of the minimum point of:

a) $y = (x + 4)^2$ b) $y = x^2 - 5$

c) $y = (x - 3)^2 - 6$ d) $y = (x + 2)^2 + 3$

Answers 4.9

d) $y = f(x + 2) + 3$; minimum point is $(-2, 3)$.

c) $y = f(x-3) - 6$; minimum point is $(3, -6)$

b) $y = f(x) - 5$; minimum point is $(0, -5)$

a) This graph is the same as $f(x + 4)$; minimum point is at $(-4, 0)$

Exercise 4.10

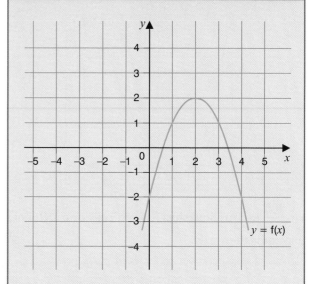

The graph above illustrates $y = f(x)$. On the same axes sketch:

1 $y = f(x + 5)$

2 $y = f(2x)$

3 $y = 2f(x)$

Answers 4.10

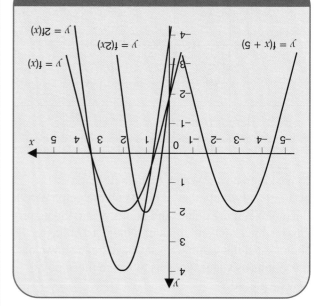

Sin, cos and tan graphs

Sine and cosine graphs have the same basic shape. The sine graph starts from the origin (remember original sin), but the cosine graph starts from 1 on the y-axis when $x = 0$ (the cos1ne graph).

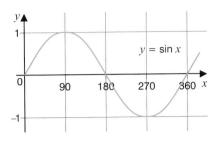

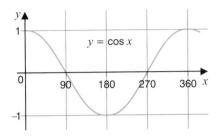

The graph of tan x is completely different, but remember that it repeats every 180°.

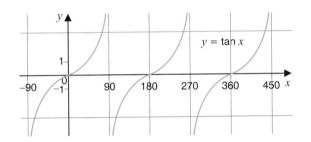

Example 4.15

Find the solutions for x in the range $0° \leqslant x < 360°$, which satisfy these equations.

a) $\sin x = 0.5$ b) $\cos x = 0.5$

c) $\cos x = 0.61$ d) $\tan x = -0.2$

Solution

a) Draw the graph of $y = \sin x$, then draw a horizontal dotted line for $y = 0.5$. This crosses the $y = \sin x$ graph at two places. The solutions are where the line cuts the graph. Using your calculator for $\sin^{-1}(0.5)$ will give you one solution i.e. 30°. The other solution is found from the graph. It is $180° - 30°$ (or $90° + 60°$) at 150°.
The solutions are $x = 30°, 150°$.

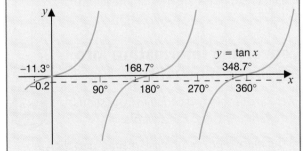

b) Draw the graph of $y = \cos x$, then draw a horizontal dotted line for $y = 0.5$.

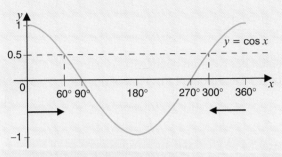

This crosses the $y = \cos x$ graph at two places, giving the two solutions.
Using your calculator for $\cos^{-1}(0.5)$ will give you one solution i.e. 60°. The other is the same distance from 360° so it is
$360° - 60° = 300°$.
The solutions are $x = 60°, 300°$.

c) Again, draw the graph of $y = \cos x$ and add a line at $y = 0.61$. The solutions are where the line cuts the graph. Your calculator will give you $\cos^{-1}(0.61) = 52.4°$. The other solution is at $360° - 52.4°$ (or $270° + 37.6°$).
The solutions are $x = 52.4°, 307.6°$.

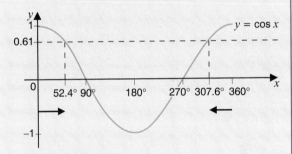

d) Draw the graph of $y = \tan x$ and then draw a horizontal dotted line for $y = -0.2$. Where this line crosses the $y = \tan x$ graph gives the solutions.

Using your calculator for $\tan^{-1}(-0.2)$ will give you $-11.3°$. This is a negative solution, and you want solutions between 0° and 360°.
Add 180° to $-11.3°$ to get 168.7°, then add 180° again to find the second solution.
The solutions are $x = 168.7°, 348.7°$.

You may have solved questions like these using the CAST diagram. If you are more at home with this method, stick with it.

```
 S | A
---+---
 T | C
```

Remember that you nearly always get more than one solution for this type of question.

Exercise 4.11

Sketch the sin, cos and tan graphs, then find all the solutions for x, correct to one decimal place, in the range $0° \leqslant x < 360°$ for the following equations.

1 $\sin x = 0.89$

2 $\tan x = -0.41$

3 $\cos x = 0.24$

4 $\sin x = -0.12$

5 $\cos x = -0.91$

Answers 4.11

5 155.5°, 204.5°

4 186.9°, 353.1°

3 76.1°, 283.9°

2 157.7°, 337.7°

1 62.9°, 117.1°

 TAKE A BREAK

All things being equal, this is a good time to take a break. Inequalities are next on the menu.

Converting information into algebraic inequalities

There are always two variables. Questions are often confusing. For example:

- *'no more than' or 'at most' means 'less than or equal to'*
- *'no less than' or 'at least' means 'more than or equal to'*

Make sure the multiple is on the correct side.

For instance, in algebra 'y is twice the size of x' becomes $y = 2x$, so 'y is at least twice the size of x' would be $y \geqslant 2x$.

Example 4.16

In the following inequalities, x represents the number of adults and y represents the number of children.

Write inequalities for each of these.

a) A stadium will seat at most 20 000 people.

b) There must be at least 5000 adults and no more than 15 000 children.

c) On average, the adults weigh 110 kg and the children weigh 55 kg. A lift can hold at most 1100 kg.

d) There should be not more than twice as many adults as children.

Solution

a) $x + y \leqslant 20\,000$

b) $x \geqslant 5000$ and $y \leqslant 15\,000$

c) $110x + 55y \leqslant 1100$

    $2x + y \leqslant 20$

    (by cancelling through by 5 and 11 or 55)

d) $x \leqslant 2y$

    (The question could be expressed as, 'The number of adults is no more than twice the number of children.')

Regions and inequalities

You may be asked to shade – or leave unshaded – the region satisfied by a number of inequalities.

For regions that include the line as part of the inequality (they involve $\geqslant$ and $\leqslant$), use a solid line. For those that exclude the line (they involve $>$ and $<$); use a broken line.

As long as the term in y is positive and on the left-hand side of the inequality, then you may use ABOVE, BELOW and BETWEEN.

So the region indicated by the inequality $y \leqslant 2x$ is BELOW the line $y = 2x$.

$3x + 4y \geqslant 24$ is the entire region ABOVE the line $3x + 4y = 24$

$0 \leqslant y \leqslant 4$ means the region BETWEEN $y = 0$ and $y = 4$

Example 4.17

The diagram below shows the graphs of $y = x$, $y = 5 - x$ and $2x + y = 10$

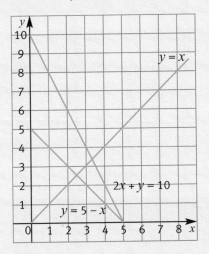

Leave unshaded the region which satisfies the following inequalities.

$y \leqslant x$

$y \geqslant 5 - x$

$2x + y \leqslant 10$

Solution

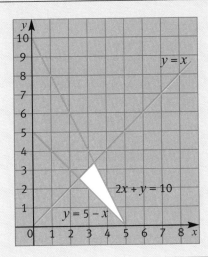

In the above inequalities, the coefficient of y is positive. Therefore:

$y \leqslant x$ is represented by the region vertically B≤LOW the line $y = x$

$y \geqslant 5 - x$ is represented by the region A≥OVE $y = 5 - x$

$2x + y \leqslant 10$ is represented by the region vertically B≤LOW $2x + y = 10$

*Usually the questions ask you to leave the required area **unshaded**, but occasionally they request the required region to be **shaded**.*

Example 4.18

A committee can have at most 20 members. Let x represent the number of men and y the number of women. Meetings are cancelled unless at least five men are present. There must be at least twice as many women as men present.

a) Find three inequalities that state the above information.

b) Show these inequalities on a graph, leaving the required region unshaded.

Solution

a) $x + y \leqslant 20$ $x \geqslant 5$ $y \geqslant 2x$ or $2x \leqslant y$

b)

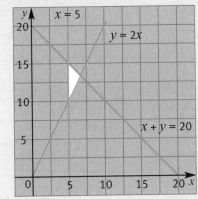

Example 4.19

A crate can hold a maximum of 40 kg of baked beans. Large cans weigh 1 kg and small cans weigh half as much. (This information is already represented on the graph as the line $2x + y = 40$, where x is the number of large cans and y is the number of small cans.)

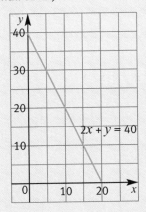

To conform with regulations, the crate cannot hold more than 15 large tins. The crate must hold no more than twice the number of small tins as large tins.

Represent this information on the graph, leaving the required area unshaded.

Solution

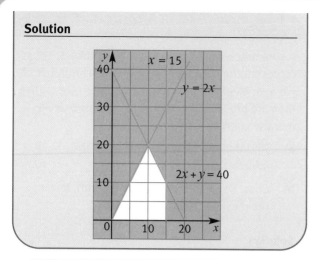

Exercise 4.12

1 A horse trader can buy up to 13 horses, but has no more than £2400 to spend. Let the number of mares be x and of stallions y. Each mare costs £240 and each stallion costs £120. He must have at least five mares and five stallions. Show the region in a graph.

2 A school teacher is planning a trip for his students. He can hire small or large minibuses. Let the number of small minibuses be x and of large minibuses be y. Each small minibus can hold 8 people, and each large minibus can hold 16. He has to carry at least 48 people, and must have at least one of each type of minibus. Show the region in a graph.

Answers 4.12

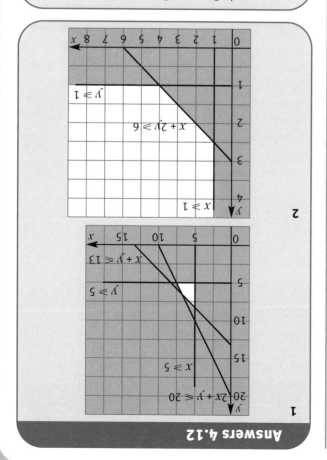

Graphs from practical situations

These are most easily solved by describing in words what happens in reality and comparing your description to the graphs given.

Drawing graphs of containers filling

When the cross-section of a container is wide, it will fill slowly; when the cross-section is narrow, it will fill quickly. To draw a graph of a container filling, write down the description of its changing cross-section next to it. If drawing a container from a graph, write down the description of the rate of incease of the graph at the bottom, middle and top. Relating this to the cross-section should enable you to draw the container.

Example 4.20

Water is poured into vases at a constant rate. Sketch the graph of the depth of water against time for the vases shown.

a)

b)

c)

Solution

a)
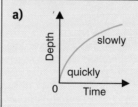

b)

c)
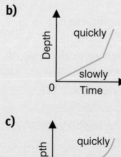

Example 4.21

Water is poured into two vases at a constant rate. The graphs for the depth of water against time are shown below.

a)

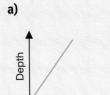

b)

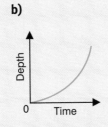

Sketch the objects that could be represented by these graphs.

Solution

a)

b)

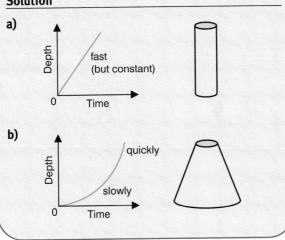

If the area of the cross-section is increasing, the rate at which the depth of liquid rises is decreasing, and vice versa.

Recognising graphs

Linear graphs

These can be written in the form $y = mx + c$ where m is the gradient and c is the y-intercept. If the gradient is positive, then the line slopes upwards from left to right:

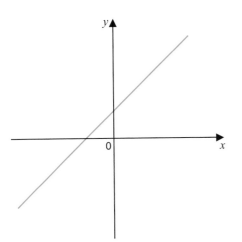

and if it is negative, then it slopes downwards.

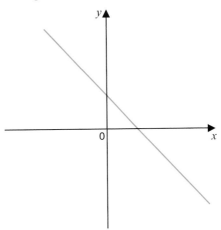

Hyperbolic graphs

Don't be put off by their name!

They are of the form $y = \dfrac{k}{x}$ where k is a constant.

e.g. $y = \dfrac{1}{x}$ which can also be written as $xy = 1$, or

$y = \dfrac{3}{x}$ which can also be written as $xy = 3$

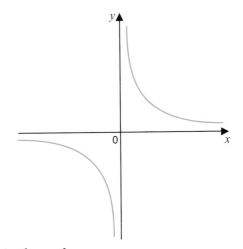

Quadratic graphs

These are written in the form $y = ax^2 + bx + c$

e.g. $y = 3x^2 - 2x + 5$

If the coefficient of x^2 is positive, then the graph looks like a smile:

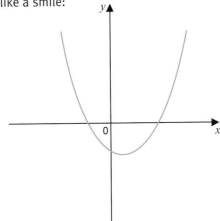

and if it is negative, then the graph looks like a sad mouth:

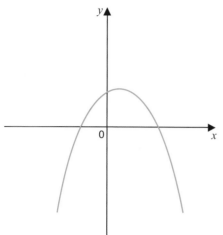

Cubic graphs

These are written in the form $y = ax^3 + bx^2 + cx + d$

e.g. $y = 3x^3 + 4x^2 - 2x - 1$

If the coefficient of x^3 is positive then, apart from a bump in it, the graph goes upwards from left to right:

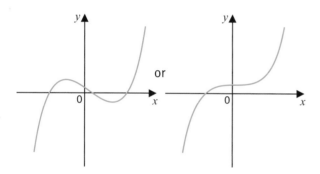

or

and if a is negative then, apart from the bump in it, the graph goes downwards from left to right.

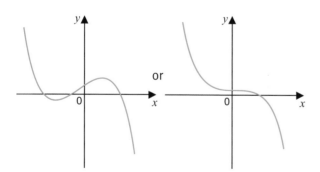

or

Circle graphs

When they are centred at the origin with radius r, the equation is $x^2 + y^2 = r^2$

 TAKE A BREAK

It's time for another break.

Exam-type questions 4

1 Find the equation of this graph.

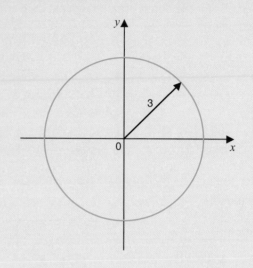

2 On graph paper, draw two axes in the ranges $-2 \leqslant x \leqslant 6$, and $-4 \leqslant y \leqslant 4$. By a graphical method, solve the following simultaneous equations.

$x + y = 2$ $y = 2x - 10$

3 Study the graphs shown. Match each graph with the equation that could represent it.

  a) $x + y = 10$ **b)** $y = \dfrac{5}{x}$

  c) $y = 10 + 9x - x^2$ **d)** $y = x^2$

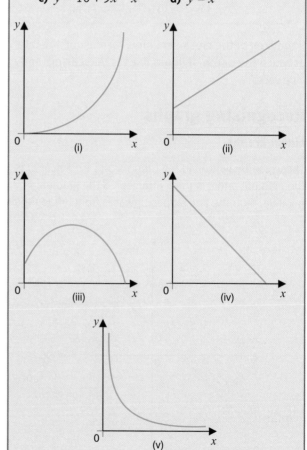

4 The diagram shows the graph of $y = f(x)$.
On the same graph, sketch the following functions.
   a) $y = f(x + 4)$ **b)** $y = f(2x)$
   c) $y = f(x) - 3$

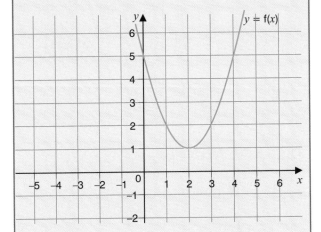

5 The graph of $y = \sin x$ is illustrated below.

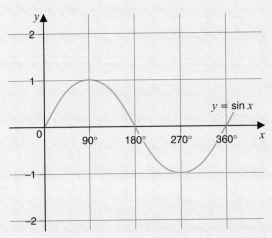

   a) Giving your answers to the nearest degree, find two solutions for the equation $\sin x = 0.67$
   b) On the same axes, sketch the curve $y = 2\sin x$

6 Find a value of x, to the nearest degree, in the range $180° < x < 360°$, such that $\cos x = 0.642$.

7 A straight line passes through the points $(0, -3)$ and $(3, 3)$.
   a) Find the gradient of the line.
   b) Find the equation of the line in the form $y = ax + b$
   c) Find the distance between the points.
   d) Find the midpoint of the points.
   e) A second line is parallel to the line and passes through $(1, 5)$. Find the equation of this line.

(**Hint:** you may find it helpful to draw a sketch of the points and the line.)

8 A concert hall can seat at most 900 people. Let x represent the number of children and y the number of adults. No more than twice as many adults as children may attend. Adults are charged £14 and children £6. At least £8400 has to be raised. Enter this information on the graph provided, shading the required region.

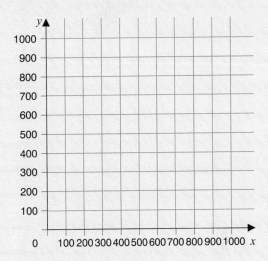

9 The graph of $y = x^3 - x$ is shown below:

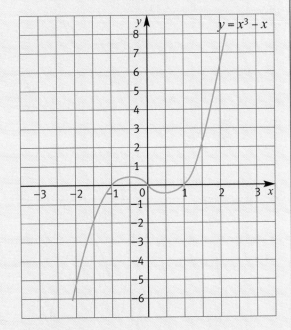

   a) Use the graph to find the solution of : $x^3 - x = 2$
   b) By adding a suitable straight line to the grid, use the graph to find the solutions of: $x^3 = 2x - 1$

63

Answers

1 $x^2 + y^2 = 9$

2 $x = 4, y = -2$

3 **a)** iv **b)** v **c)** iii **d)** i

4

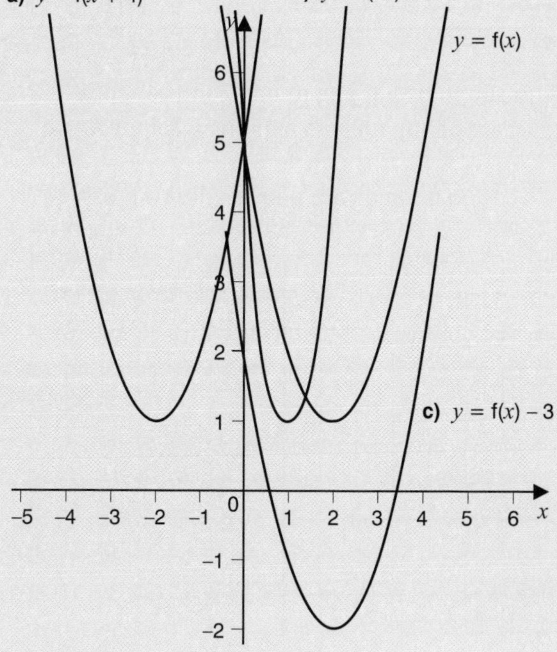

a) y = f(x + 4)
b) y = f(2x)
y = f(x)
c) y = f(x) – 3
x
y

5 **a)** 42° and 138°

b)

y = 2 sin x
y = sin x
90°
180°
270°
360°
x
y

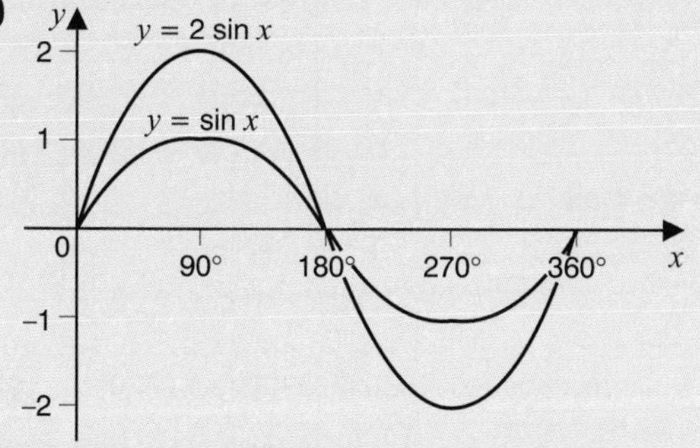

6 310° Hint: Sketch $y = \cos x$

7 **a)** 2 **b)** $y = 2x - 3$ **c)** $\sqrt{45}$ or 6.7 (1 d.p.)

d) (1.5, 0) **e)** $y = 2x + 3$

8 $6x + 14y \geq 8400$, $x + y \leq 900$, $y \leq 2x$

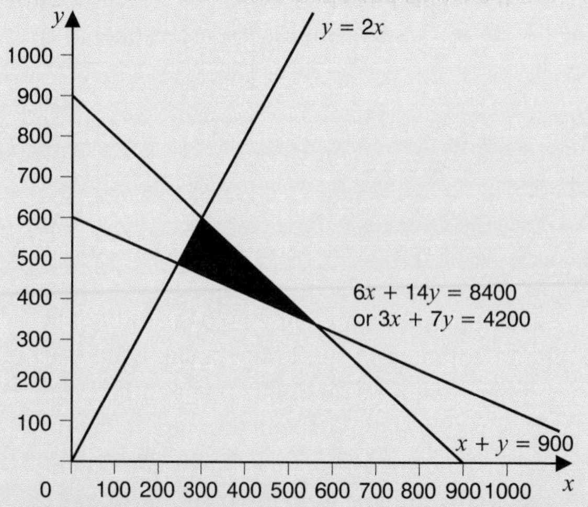

y = 2x
6x + 14y = 8400
or 3x + 7y = 4200
x + y = 900
x
y

9 **a)** Add the line $y = 2$ to the grid. This crosses the curve where $x = 1.5$.

b) **i)** Start with the original equation, $x^3 = 2x - 1$.

ii) The equation should be arranged to have $x^3 - x$ on one side.

$$x^3 = 2x - 1$$
$$\frac{-x}{x^3 - x} = \frac{-x}{x - 1}$$

iii) Therefore $y = x - 1$ should be drawn on the grid to solve the given equation.

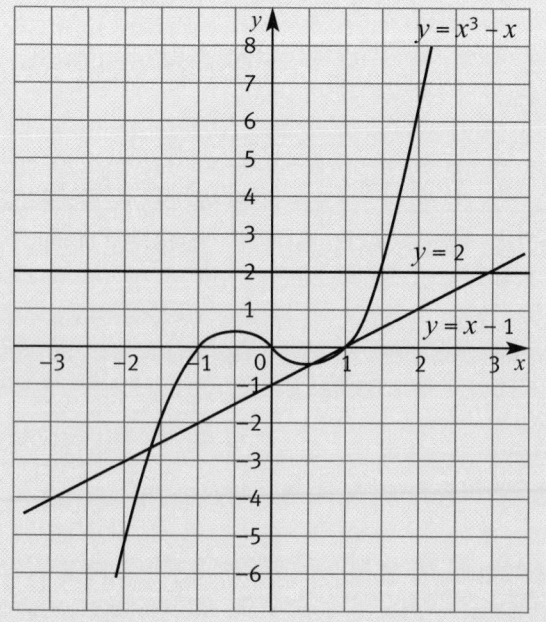

y = x³ – x
y = 2
y = x – 1
x
y

Solutions are $x = -1.6, 0.6, 1$. Your answer should be close to these but do not need to be exactly the same.

REVIEW

How much have you learnt?
Tick off each topic in the list when you are confident that you can cope with it.

- ☐ **Identify the gradient and *y*-intercept from the equation of a straight line.**
- ☐ **Solve simultaneous equations graphically.**
- ☐ **Sketch graphs of quadratic equations.**
- ☐ **Convert a non-linear graph to a linear graph by changing variables.**
- ☐ **Find values of the constants in a non-linear function.**
- ☐ **Transform functions.**
- ☐ **Draw trigonometric graphs.**
- ☐ **Find the values of an unknown, in a given range, that satisfy a trigonometric equation.**
- ☐ **Find a range of values that satisfy an algebraic inequality.**
- ☐ **Maximise or minimise an expression.**
- ☐ **Recognise graphs of mathematical equations.**

PREVIEW

By the end of this chapter you will be able to:

• identify and label angles

• recognise the rules for congruency in triangles

• identify similar triangles

• identify and calculate interior angles and exterior angles

• construct a perpendicular bisector of a line, draw a perpendicular from a point to a line

• construct an angle of 90°, an angle of 60°, bisect an angle

• construct simple loci.

Things you should know

Triangles

• Scalene triangle: one with all sides and all angles different.
• Isosceles triangle: one with two sides and two angles equal.
• Equilateral triangle: one with all sides equal and all angles 60°.

Angles

• Acute: $0° < x < 90°$
• Obtuse: $90° < x < 180°$
• Reflex: $180° < x < 360°$

Labelling angles

The angle marked at C may be called angle ACD or angle DCA. In some books this is written ∠ACD, ∠DCA, AĈD or DĈA.

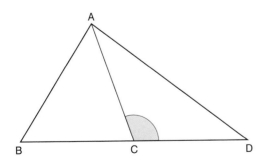

The marked angle at C is formed by two lines AC and CD. To name the angle, you follow the line from A to C to D or vice versa. This is to avoid confusion with the other angle at C running from A to C to B, or vice versa – which is called ∠ACB or ∠BCA.

Triangles

Congruent triangles

Congruent triangles are identical in size and shape, although you may have to flip one over or turn it around for the two to appear to fit on top of each other.

Rules for congruency

1 SAS – side, angle, side – two sides and the angle in between are the same

2 AAS – angle, angle, side – two angles and the **corresponding** side are the same

3 SSS – all three sides are the same

4 HRS – hypotenuse, right angle and side are the same

Exercise 5.1

Are these pairs of triangles definitely congruent? If so, give a reason for your answer.

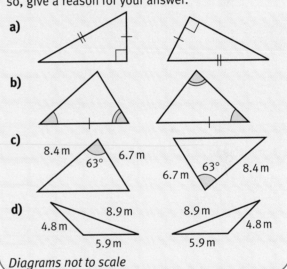

a)

b)

c) 8.4 m 63° 6.7 m   6.7 m 63° 8.4 m

d) 8.9 m 4.8 m 5.9 m   8.9 m 4.8 m 5.9 m

Diagrams not to scale

Answers 5.1

a) Yes, HRS

b) No – the given side is not opposite the same angle in the two triangles

c) Yes, SAS   d) Yes, SSS

Similar triangles

These triangles have identical angles, but one is an enlargement of the other. Try using X-Direct to find lengths of sides in similar triangles.

Note: The words 'congruent' and 'similar' can describe any group of shapes, but are usually applied to triangles.

Shapes and constructions

Exercise 5.2

1 Z is a point on the side AB of the square ABCD. BX is perpendicular to CZ, and DY is perpendicular to CZ. Prove that ΔCYD is congruent to ΔBCX.

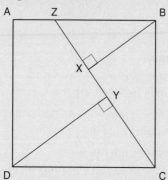

2 In the diagram below, name:
  a) two triangles that are congruent
  b) two triangles that are similar.
  Give reasons for your answer.

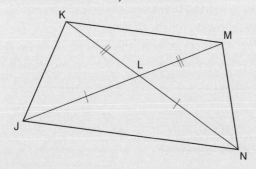

3 ΔADE and ΔBCE are similar. Find:
  a) AE   **b)** BE.

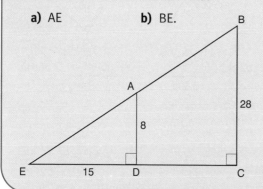

Exterior and interior angles of a regular polygon

Exterior angles

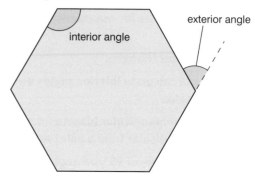

An exterior angle of an *n*-sided regular polygon
$= \dfrac{360°}{n}$

Interior angles

1 Find the exterior angle by using 360° ÷ *n*

2 As the interior and exterior angles lie on a straight line, they add up to 180°.

Interior angle = 180° − exterior angle

The angle in the centre of a regular polygon is the same as the exterior angle.

Exercise 5.3

1 A regular polygon has an interior angle of 120°.
  a) Find its exterior angle.
  b) How many sides does it have?

2 Find the exterior and interior angles of a regular octagon.

3 A regular polygon has an exterior angle of 36°. Find:
  a) the interior angle
  b) the number of sides
  c) the sum of the interior angles.

Answers 5.2

1 BC = CD
Angles YDC + YCD = 90°
Angles BCY + YCD = 90°
Therefore angle YDC = angle BCY
Therefore the triangles are congruent (AAS)

2 Congruent triangles are JKL and LMN (SAS)
Similar triangles are KLM and JLN – both are isosceles with the same angle at L.

3 a) AE = 17 (Pythagoras)   **b)** BE = 59.5

Answers 5.3

1 a) 180° − 120° = 60°
  b) 360 ÷ 60 = 6 sides

2 Exterior angle = $\dfrac{360°}{8}$ = 45°
Interior angle = 180° − 45° = 135°

3 a) 180° − 36° = 144°
  b) 360° ÷ 36 = 10 sides
  c) 144 × 10 = 1440°

Loci and constructions

Whenever drawing loci and constructions, always leave your construction lines on, so that the examiner can tell that you have used the right method.

Loci are lines or curves which join up a group of points. The points are usually described by a rule. The line or curve is called a locus, and 'loci' is the plural form.

Perpendicular bisector

The perpendicular bisector is a line which cuts a line in half and is perpendicular to it. It is also equidistant (i.e. the same distance) from the end points.

PerpendicuLar: at right angles L
Bisect: cut in half

Drawing the perpendicular bisector

Example 5.1

The rail track has to run in between two towns, A and B. It must be built so that wherever the train stops, it will be equidistant from both towns. Draw a plan of the route of the rail track.

Solution

1 Put the point of your compasses on one end of the line between A and B and open the compasses to a radius which is more than half the length of the line.

2 Using only light pressure, draw an arc either side of the line.

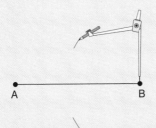

3 Without changing the radius, draw arcs from the other end. Join the two crosses to make the perpendicular bisector.

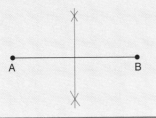

Constructing an angle of 90°

Use the perpendicular bisector method described above.

Constructing an angle of 60°

This is the same as the method used for constructing equilateral triangles.

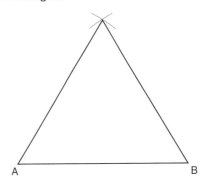

Using any line AB, set your compasses to the same length as AB. Put the point on A and draw an arc, and repeat for B. A line from either end point of AB to this arc makes an angle of 60° with AB.

Constructing other angles

To construct angles of 45° and 30°, bisect the angles of 90° and 60° respectively.

Do not use compasses if the joint is loose, and always hold them from the top. The radius must be the same from both ends of the line.

Drawing the shortest distance from a point to a line, or drawing a perpendicular from a line to a point

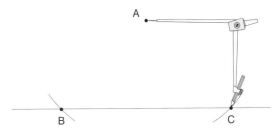

Set your compasses to any length and draw an arc from A, cutting the line twice. The two points of intersection of the arc and line are labelled as B and C. Draw the perpendicular bisector between these points to A. This line, at right angles to BC, gives the shortest distance from BC to A.

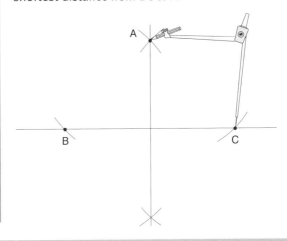

Bisecting an angle

Example 5.2

A path runs between the two straight roads, OA and OB. The path bisects the angle between the roads. Show this on a diagram.

Solution

1   Put the point of the compasses on the point of the angle and make an arc on each arm, C and D.

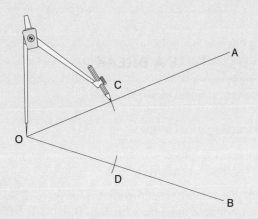

2   Move the point of the compasses to C and D in turn and make a further arc from each. Do not change the radius between drawing from C and drawing from D.

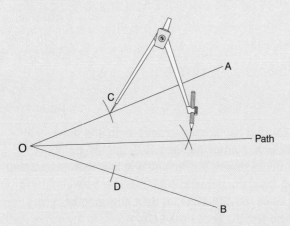

3   Join the cross to the point of the angle to make the bisector of the angle.

Loci

The path of a moving particle that is always a fixed distance from a point will give a circle, with the point at the centre and the distance as the radius.

The path of a particle that stays a fixed distance away from a line is a line parallel to it.

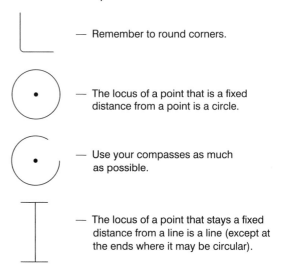

— Remember to round corners.

— The locus of a point that is a fixed distance from a point is a circle.

— Use your compasses as much as possible.

— The locus of a point that stays a fixed distance from a line is a line (except at the ends where it may be circular).

Example 5.3

Radio masts stand on each of three hills, A, B and C. They can transmit over distances of 90 km, 105 km and 120 km respectively. Shade on the diagram below the area covered by all three masts, using a scale of 1 cm : 30 km.

Solution

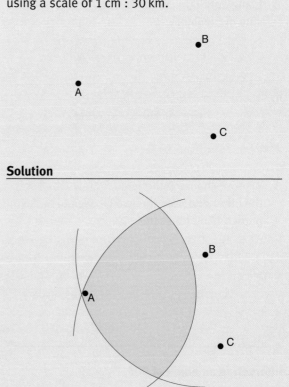

Example 5.4

A triangular field is pictured below. When a fire is burning in the field, its smoke can be seen up to 2 kilometres away. Using a scale of 1 cm : 1 km, indicate on the diagram below the region in which the smoke can be seen.

Hint: Be careful to round the corners using compasses.

Solution

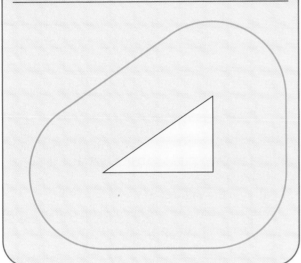

Exercise 5.4

Trace the diagram below and draw:

1 the perpendicular bisector of AB

2 the locus of the point equidistant from AB and AD

3 the locus of the point 2 cm outside ABCD.

Show all your construction lines.

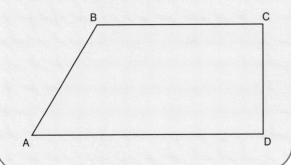

Answers 5.4

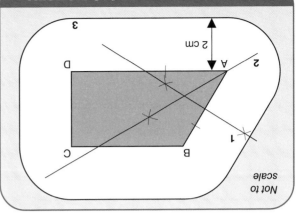

Not to scale

TAKE A BREAK

Take a break before you tackle the exam-type questions. There has been more than you would think in this chapter.

Exam-type questions 5

The diagrams below are not drawn to scale.

1 All of these triangles are similar. Calculate:
   a) x **b)** y

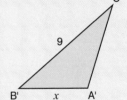
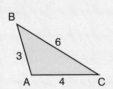
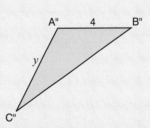

2 A helicopter pad is pictured below. Rotors can extend up to 2.5 m beyond the body of a helicopter. Draw the region around the pad where it would be unsafe to walk, using a scale of 1 cm : 2 m.

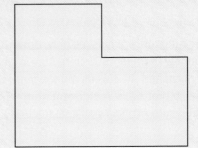

3 a) Explain why triangles PQT and RST are similar.

b) Find PT.

c) Find RS.

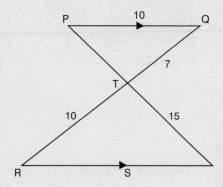

4 ABCDE is a regular pentagon. Find:

a) ∠EAB

b) ∠EBC

c) ∠CAB

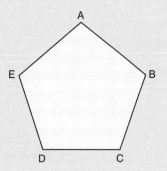

5 Using ruler and compasses only and showing all constructions, draw the shortest line from X to AB.

X

A ——————————————————————— B

6 Using ruler and compasses only, draw accurately triangle ABC where AB = 4 cm, BC = 5 cm and AC = 6 cm. Mark a point D on BC, such that AD is equidistant from AB and AC. Measure AD. Show all constructions.

7 Using ruler and compasses only, draw a point C above the horizontal line AB so that angle CAB = 90° and angle ABC = 60°. Show all constructions.

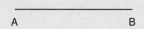

A ——————————— B

8 The diagram shows part of a regular *n*-sided polygon.
a) Find the value of *r*.
b) Hence find the number of sides of the complete polygon.

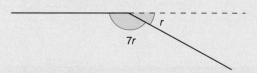

9 State, with reasons, whether the following pairs of triangles are necessarily congruent.

a)

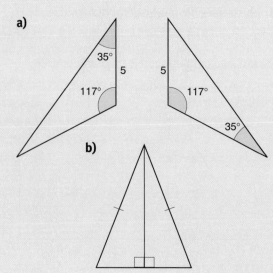

b)

c)

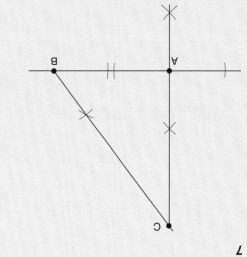

10 In the triangle below QT and RS are parallel.

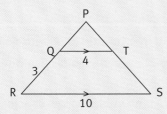

a) Explain why triangles PQT and PRS are similar.

b) Find length PQ.

5

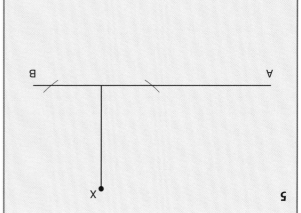

6 AD = 4.4 cm

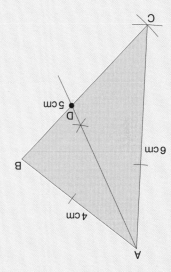

7

8 $r = 22.5°$, $n = 16$

9 a) not congruent (not AAS because the sides are not corresponding)

b) congruent (isosceles triangles can be confirmed by any rule)

c) not congruent (although it appears SAS, the angles do not correspond)

Answers

1 a) 4.5 **b)** $5\frac{1}{3}$ or 5.333

2

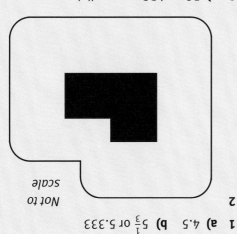

Not to scale

3 a) PQ and RS are parallel so
∠RTS = ∠PTQ (opposite angles);
∠RTS = ∠RST, ∠PQT = ∠SRT
(alternate angles), as all the related angles are identical the triangles are similar.

b) PT = 10.5

c) RS = 14.3

4 a) 108° (using $\frac{360}{n}$ etc.)

b) 72° (angles of quadrilateral EBCD add up to 360°)

c) 36° (triangle EAB is isosceles)

Shapes and constructions

10 a) The angles in the triangles are the same because of corresponding angles (at Q and R, and at T and S).

b) $\dfrac{PR}{RS} = \dfrac{PQ}{QT}$

Let PQ = x. Then

$$\dfrac{x + 3}{x} = \dfrac{10}{4}$$

$$\dfrac{x + 3}{x} = \dfrac{5}{2}$$

$$2(x + 3) = 5x$$

PQ = x = 2

REVIEW

How much have you learnt?
Tick off each topic in the list when you are confident that you can cope with it.

- ☐ Identify and label angles.
- ☐ Recognise the rules for congruency in triangles.
- ☐ Identify congruent triangles.
- ☐ Identify similar triangles.
- ☐ Identify interior angles, exterior angles.
- ☐ Construct a perpendicular line from a line to a point.
- ☐ Construct a perpendicular bisector of a line, a perpendicular from a point to a line.
- ☐ Construct an angle of 90° an angle of 60°, bisect an angle.
- ☐ Construct simple loci.

PREVIEW

By the end of this chapter you will be able to:

- solve trigonometric problems involving sine, cosine and tangent of an angle
- find missing lengths in a right-angled triangle
- solve problems in 3D trigonometry
- use the sine rule and cosine rule with scalene non-right-angled triangles.

Pythagoras – a reminder

$a^2 + b^2 = c^2$

$a^2 = c^2 - b^2$

$b^2 = c^2 - a^2$

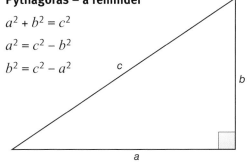

Exercise 6.1

1 Find the length labelled x on the triangles below:

a)

2.9

x

4.6

b)

5.3

x

8.9

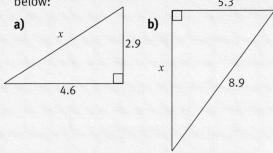

2 Is the triangle below a right-angled triangle? Give a reason for your answer.

9.6

4.9

6.2

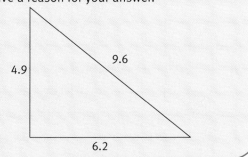

Answers 6.1

1 a) $\sqrt{4.6^2 + 2.9^2} = 5.4$ (1 d.p.)

b) $\sqrt{8.9^2 - 5.3^2} = 7.1$ (1 d.p.)

2 No – because $4.9^2 + 6.2^2$ does not equal 9.6^2.

Trigonometry

Always make sure that your calculator is set to degrees before you start, or all your answers will be wrong!

You may have learnt the trigonometry rules by a method different from the one we suggest below. If you are happy with your own method, skip to Example 6.1.

If not, try the following method using SOH CAH TOA.

If you are having trouble remembering SOH CAH TOA, try:

Some Old Hags Can't Always Hide Their Old Age.

Use triplets, putting the **middle** letter to the top of the triplet.

S: $\sin \theta = \dfrac{\text{opp}}{\text{hyp}}$

O: opp $= \sin \theta \times$ hyp

H: hyp $= \dfrac{\text{opp}}{\sin \theta}$

C: $\cos \theta = \dfrac{\text{adj}}{\text{hyp}}$

A: adj $= \cos \theta \times$ hyp

H: hyp $= \dfrac{\text{adj}}{\cos \theta}$

T: $\tan \theta = \dfrac{\text{opp}}{\text{adj}}$

O: opp $= \tan \theta \times$ adj

A: adj $= \dfrac{\text{opp}}{\tan \theta}$

Put your finger over or cross out the relevant letter.

We often use the Greek letter θ (theta) for angles.

Procedure for solving trigonometry problems

1 *Write out SOH CAH TOA in triplet form, putting the middle letter at the top.*

2 *Which sides are mentioned in the question? (If it helps, label the sides.) If you are asked to find a side, include this as being mentioned in the question.*

3 *Put your finger over or cross out the letter you want to find, and this will give you the formula.*

This might sound confusing at first, but if you work through the following examples, everything will become clear.

Pythagoras' theorem and trigonometry

Example 6.1

Find the angle labelled θ in the triangle below.

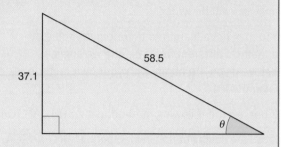

Solution

This question includes the opposite (opp) and hypotenuse (hyp), so use SOH. Drawing out the triplet gives:

$$\sin \theta = \frac{\text{opp}}{\text{hyp}} = \frac{37.1}{58.5}$$

$$\sin \theta = 0.6342$$

To find the angle, you need its inverse (in this case, inverse sin or $\sin^{-1}$).

$$\theta = \sin^{-1}(0.6342)$$
$$= 39.4° \text{ correct to 1 d.p.}$$

If you are getting an Error sign on your calculator or a ridiculous answer, you are probably not pressing `=` before you press `INV` `SIN`, `COS` or `TAN`. Also, some calculators require you to press `=` at the end, or use brackets, so it's a good idea to find out in good time how yours works. If you still can't find out where you went wrong, check that your calculator is set to degrees!

Example 6.2

Find the length labelled x in the triangle.

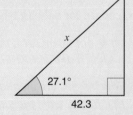

Solution

Using

$$\text{hyp} = \frac{\text{adj}}{\cos\theta}$$

$$x = \frac{42.3}{\cos 27.1°}$$

$$x = 47.5 \text{ (correct to 1 d.p.)}$$

What about isosceles triangles?

To make an isosceles triangle into two right-angled triangles, draw a line from the middle of the unequal side to the opposite vertex. This is a perpendicular bisector.

Angles of elevation and depression

Angles of **elevation** and **depression** must be measured from the horizontal. You look at the horizon and move your head **up** for an angle of elevation or **down** for an angle of depression.

3D trigonometry

The secret of working in 3D is to find a right-angled triangle. If one is not obvious, draw a line from the starting point to the peak or top point of the 'solid' shape. From there, draw another line vertically down, and join the point where it hits the ground, directly beneath, to your starting point. You should now have a right-angled triangle. You may need to use Pythagoras' theorem as well as trigonometry.

The most usual questions involve pyramids, wedges or cuboids.

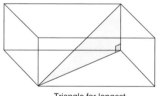

Triangle for longest length in a cuboid

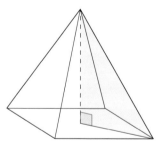

Triangle for questions involving an edge and plane

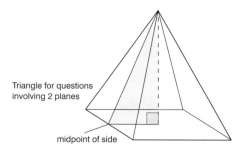

Triangle for questions involving 2 planes

midpoint of side

Example 6.3

The diagram shows a square-based pyramid. The point P is directly above the centre of the square, X. E is the midpoint of AD.
AD = 5.6 m and
PX = 7.2 m.

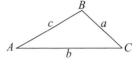

a) Find the angle PDX.

b) Find the length of PD.

c) Find the angle PEX.

Solution

a) $BD = \sqrt{5.6^2 + 5.6^2} = 7.92$ m

$DX = 7.92 \div 2 = 3.96$

$\angle PDX = \tan^{-1}(7.2 \div 3.96) = 61.2°$

b) $PD = 8.2$ m (Use $\triangle PXD$)

c) $\angle PEX = \tan^{-1}(7.2 \div 2.8) = 68.7°$

Example 6.4

Timber is stored in a cuboid-shaped barn. Find the longest possible length of timber that would fit in the barn.

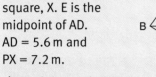

Solution

The longest piece of timber would go from a vertex (corner) at the bottom to a diagonally opposite vertex at the top.

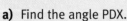

Find the length of the diagonal on the base:
$\sqrt{6^2 + 4^2} = 7.2$ m

Length of the longest piece of timber:
$\sqrt{7.2^2 + 3.5^2} = 8.0$ m

Trigonometry for non-right angled scalene triangles

Scalene triangles have no sides equal. There are two rules for non-right-angled scalene triangles: the sine and the cosine rule. These formulae are usually given on the *Information and formulae sheet*.

How do I know which rule to use?

Remember how to label triangles.

*Remember **SALSA CLASS**.*

The **S**ine rule links an **A**ngle, **L**ength, **S**ide and an **A**ngle.

The **C**osine rule links a **L**ength, **A**ngle, **S**ide and another **S**ide.

The sine rule

This rule is used when the question involves two angles and two lengths.

This version of the formula is easier to use for finding angles:

$$\frac{\sin A}{a} = \frac{\sin B}{b} = \frac{\sin C}{c}$$

and this one is easier for finding lengths:

$$\frac{a}{\sin A} = \frac{b}{\sin B} = \frac{c}{\sin C}$$

The cosine rule

This rule applies when you are working with three lengths and one angle.

To find length a: $a^2 = b^2 + c^2 - 2bc \cos A$

To find angle A: $\cos A = \dfrac{b^2 + c^2 - a^2}{2bc}$

and use **SHIFT** (or **2nd f**) **COS** to find the angle.

Can you work out the formulae for sides b and c, and for angles B and C?

Exercise 6.2

Find the lengths or angles marked x in the following triangles:

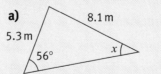

Diagrams not to scale

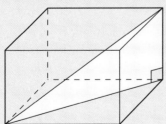

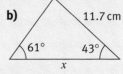

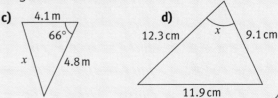

Answers 6.2

a) $\dfrac{\sin x}{5.3} = \dfrac{\sin 56°}{8.1} \Rightarrow \sin x = 0.542 \Rightarrow x = 33°$

b) The angle opposite the side x is
$180 - (61 + 43) = 76°$
$\dfrac{x}{\sin 76°} = \dfrac{11.7}{\sin 61°} \Rightarrow x = \dfrac{11.7}{\sin 61°} \times \sin 76°$
$\Rightarrow x = 13.0\ \text{cm}$

c) It does not matter whether $b = 4.1$ and $c = 4.8$ or $b = 4.8$ and $c = 4.1$
$x^2 = 4.1^2 + 4.8^2 - 2 \times 4.1 \times 4.8 \times \cos 66°$
$\Rightarrow x^2 = 23.84 \Rightarrow x = 4.9\ \text{m}$

d) It is important to label the side opposite the angle as a, or 11.9. Then b and c are 12.3 and 9.1, but it does not matter which way round these are substituted.
$\cos x = \dfrac{12.3^2 + 9.1^2 - 11.9^2}{2 \times 12.3 \times 9.1}$
$\Rightarrow x = \text{inv cos}(0.413) = 66°$

Sine rule – the ambiguous case

When using the sine rule, you sometimes get two possible answers.

Example 6.5

In the triangle ABC, angle ABC = 41°, AB = 6.5 cm, AC = 5.5 cm. Find the possible sizes of angle ACB to 1 decimal place.

Solution

There are two triangles that satisfy these measurements:

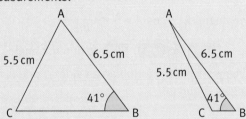

So there are two possible sizes of angle ACB.
Let angle ACB = x

Using the sine rule, $\dfrac{\sin x}{6.5} = \dfrac{\sin 41}{5.5}$

$\sin x = 0.775\ldots$

There are two possible solutions

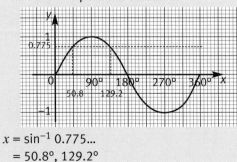

$x = \sin^{-1} 0.775\ldots$
$= 50.8°,\ 129.2°$

Finding the area of any triangle

Starting from the sine rule, by a complicated process, it is possible to find the formula for the area of any triangle. You do not need to know the process, but you should learn the rule.

Area of triangle ABC
$= \frac{1}{2}ab \sin C = \frac{1}{2}bc \sin A = \frac{1}{2}ac \sin B$

Exercise 6.3

In this exercise, it may help to sketch the triangles first.

1. In the triangle ABC, angle ABC = 62°, AB = 7.8 cm, AC = 6.9 cm. Find the possible sizes of angle ACB to 1 decimal place.

2. In the triangle PQR, angle PQR = 55°, PQ = 10.8 cm, PR = 8.9 cm. Find the possible sizes of angle PRQ correct to 1 decimal place.

Answers 6.3

1 86.5°, 93.5°   2 83.7°, 96.3°

The four points of bearings

1. Always start where you want the bearing 'from'.
2. Then look north.
3. Always turn clockwise.
4. Always use three figures to write the bearing.

Example 6.5

An aeroplane flies in a straight line from point A, on a bearing of 048°, for 280 km. It lands at point B. It then takes off again and flies for 190 km on a bearing of 187°, to land at point C.

a) Find the direct distance of C from A.

b) Find the bearing of C from A.

Solution

Draw a diagram.

To find the angle at B, remember that the angles at a point add up to 360°.

Then angle ABC
$= 360° - (180° - 48°) - 187°$
$= 41°$

a) To find the length AC, use the cosine rule.
$AC^2 = 280^2 + 190^2 - 2 \times 280 \times 190 \times \cos 41°$
$= 34\,198.9$
$AC = 184.9\ \text{km (1 d.p.)}$

b) To find angle BAC, use the sine rule.

$$\frac{\sin BAC}{190} = \frac{\sin 41°}{184.9}$$

$$\sin BAC = 190 \times \frac{\sin 41°}{184.9}$$

$$= 0.674\ 154\ 762$$

angle BAC = 42.4°

The bearing of C from A is 48° + 42.4° = 090.4° (1 d.p.)

Exercise 6.4

1 Using the triangle below, find:
a) BD **b)** CD.

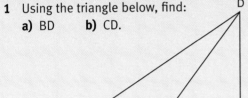

2 Dylan is lost. He walks 6.2 km on a bearing of 111°. He then changes direction and walks 5.9 km on a bearing of 348°. Using trigonometry, find his distance (to the nearest 0.1 kilometre) and the bearing from his original point (to the nearest degree).

3 Andy stands at a point C at the top of a vertical cliff. Laura in a canoe at B sees Andy at C, a distance of 210 m away. Laura is 156 m from the base of the cliff, A. What is the angle of depression of Laura from Andy?

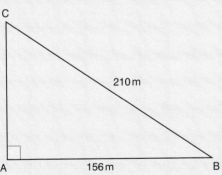

4 In the diagram below find:
a) the length marked x
b) the angle y.

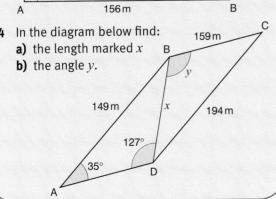

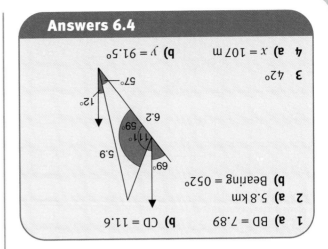
If a shape is unlabelled, it often helps to label the vertices yourself. This makes it easier to refer to the angle or side that you are using.

STOP **TAKE A BREAK**

Still bearing up? Take a break before you check out the rest of this chapter.

Exam-type questions 6

Unless otherwise stated, all lengths are in centimetres.

1 Find x in the following.

a)

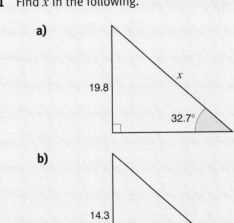

b)

c)

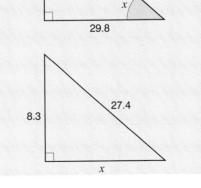

2 Is the angle at B a right angle, acute or obtuse?

a)

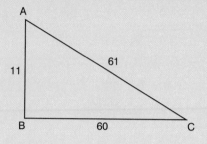

b)

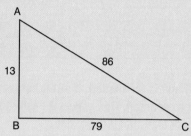

c)

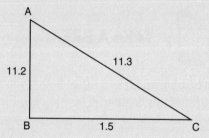

3 a) What is the name given to this type of triangle?

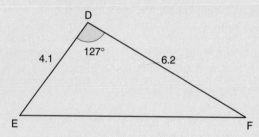

b) Find EF.

4 A is a point at the top of a vertical cliff 20 m high. The angle of depression from A to a point C is 57°. Calculate BC.

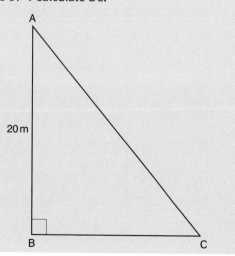

5 A, B and C are three towers. B is on a bearing of 250° from C and 8 km away from it. C is on a bearing of 051° and 30 km from A.

a) Calculate AB.

b) Calculate the bearing of B from A.

c) Taking 1 km to equal $\frac{5}{8}$ mile give the distance AB in miles.

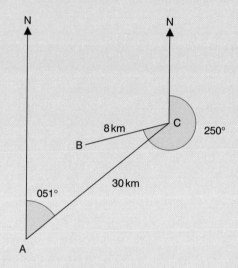

6 In the triangle PQS, find:

a) PS

b) RQ

c) angle RPQ.

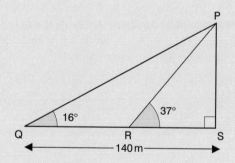

7 In the triangle JKL, find:

a) JL

b) KL

c) the area.

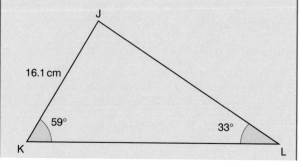

8 A tanker is at a bearing of 117° from a port, and a lighthouse is at a bearing of 261° from the tanker and 197° from the port. The distance of the lighthouse from the port is 562 m. Find:

a) angle PTL

b) the distance of the lighthouse from the tanker.

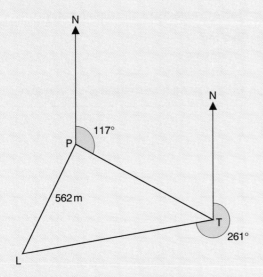

9 In the triangle ABC, calculate:

a) the perpendicular height from C to AB produced (extended)

b) the area of triangle ABC

c) the length of BC.

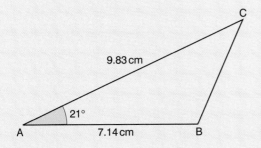

10 AO represents a tree 10.6 m tall. Two people standing at B and C respectively are looking at the top of the tree. The angle of elevation from B to the top of the tree is 35° and from C is 52°. Find:

a) OB

b) OC

c) BC.

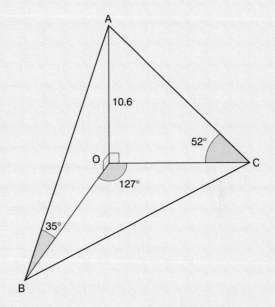

11 The diagram shows a square-based pyramid with a vertical height AX of 22.6 cm and a base of side 15 cm. Find:

a) the length of AD

b) angle ADX

c) the angle between the plane ABE and the base.

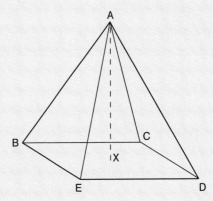

12 A box in the shape of a cuboid has width 28 cm, depth 14 cm and height 11 cm. What is the longest pencil that would fit in the box?

Answers

1 **a)** 36.7 cm   **b)** 26°   **c)** 26.1 cm

2 **a)** 90°   **b)** obtuse   **c)** 90°

3 **a)** non-right angled scalene (i.e. all 3 sides different lengths)
   b) 9.3 to 1 d.p.

4 (Remember that the angles of depression are measured from the horizontal.) 13.0 m

5 **a)** 22.6 km   **b)** 044°   **c)** 14.1 miles

6 **a)** 40.14
   b) RQ = 140 − 53.3 = 86.7 (RS = 53.3)
   c) 21° (It is easier to use the fact that the angles of a triangle add to 180°.)

7 **a)** 25.3 cm   **b)** 29.5 cm   **c)** 204 cm^2

8 **a)** 36°   **b)** 942 m

9 **a)** 3.52 cm   **b)** 12.6 cm^2 **c)** 4.07 cm

10 **a)** 15.14 m   **b)** 8.28 m   **c)** 21.2 m

11 **a)** 24.97 (using Pythagoras' theorem, X is the midpoint of BD, XD = 10.6)
   b) 65° to the nearest degree
   c) $\tan^{-1}$ (22.6 ÷ 7.5) = 72° to the nearest degree

12 The longest pencil is the hypotenuse of the shaded triangle.

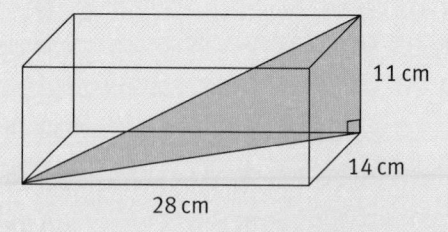

Longest dimension on the base = $\sqrt{28^2 + 14^2}$
  = 31.30 cm

Longest possible pencil = $\sqrt{31.30^2 + 11^2}$
  = 33.2 cm

REVIEW

How much have you learnt?
Tick off each topic in the list when you are confident that you can cope with it.

- ☐ Solve trigonometric problems involving sine, cosine and tangent of an angle.
- ☐ Find missing lengths in a right-angled triangle.
- ☐ Solve problems in 3D trigonometry.
- ☐ Use the
  - ☐ sine rule
  - ☐ cosine rule
  with scalene non-right-angled triangles.

Pythagoras' theorem and trigonometry

For example, a solid cylinder

$$= 2 \text{ circles} + 1 \text{ rectangle} = 2\pi r^2 + 2\pi r h$$

Check if the hollow cylinder or cuboid has a lid.

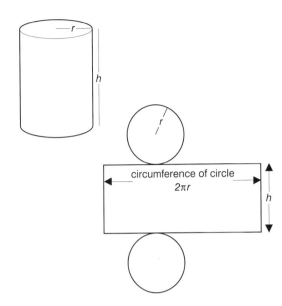

Area

Area of a triangle

In a triangle, if you know the base and perpendicular height (or the equivalent turned around), you can use:

area of a triangle $= \frac{1}{2} \times$ base $\times$ height

If not, you must use:

area $= \frac{1}{2}ab \sin C$

This will probably be on your *Information and formulae sheet*.

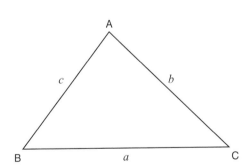

Area and circumference of a circle

'πr *squarea gives you the area*', πr^2

Remember 'squarea'.

$2\pi r$ (or πd) gives the circumference.

Surface area of 3D shapes

Imagine your 3D shape opened out into a net, then describe the shape of each of the pieces. By finding the areas of these pieces and adding them, you can find the total surface area of the shape.

Volume

Volume of a prism (sometimes called a right prism)

A prism is a 3D shape which you can cut into identical slices.

For example, if you slice a cylinder, each piece is a circle.

The name given to the shape of each slice is the **cross-section**.

The volume of a prism is area of cross-section × length.

V stands for volume. The word 'volume' is usually used, but occasionally you may be asked for capacity.

A stands for the area of the cross-section.

L stands for length.

But remember you may not be asked for the length. Instead you may be asked for a width, depth, height or thickness.

Volume and surface area of cones and spheres

Volume of a cone of base radius r and height $h = \frac{1}{3}\pi r^2 h$

Volume of a sphere of radius $r = \frac{4}{3}\pi r^3$

Curved surface area of a cone $= \pi r l$ where l is the slant height.

Surface area of a sphere of radius $r = 4\pi r^2$

Example 7.1

a) A toy is made from a hollow hemisphere and a cone, as shown.

   i) Find the volume of the object.

   ii) Find the surface area of the object.

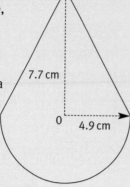

7.7 cm

0   4.9 cm

b) The toy stands on its hemispherical base, with the cone vertical. Sand fills the toy to a horizontal level 6.1 cm from the bottom of the toy. Find the volume of sand used.

Solution

a) i) Volume of hemisphere $= \frac{4}{3}\pi(4.9)^3 \div 2$

$= 246.4 \text{ cm}^3$

Volume of cone $= \frac{1}{3}\pi(4.9)^2(7.7)$

$= 193.6 \text{ cm}^3$

Total volume $= 440 \text{ cm}^3$

ii) Slant height $l = \sqrt{4.9^2 + 7.7^2}$

$= 9.13 \text{ cm}$

Surface area of conical part $= \pi \times 4.9 \times 9.13$

$= 140.5 \text{ cm}^2$

Surface area of hemisphere $= 4 \times \pi \times 4.9^2 \div 2$

$= 150.9 \text{ cm}^2$

Total surface area $= 140.5 + 150.9 = 291.4 \text{ cm}^2$

b) The sand fills the cone up to 1.2 cm from the base.

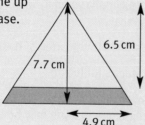

6.5 cm

7.7 cm

4.9 cm

The height of the unfilled cone = 6.5 cm.

Using similar triangles, the radius of the unfilled volume is $4.9 \div 7.7 \times 6.5 = 4.1364 \text{ cm}$

Unfilled volume of the cone $= \frac{1}{3}\pi(4.1364)^2(6.5)$

$= 116.5 \text{ cm}^3$

Volume of sand $= 246.4 + 193.6 - 116.5$

$= 323.5 \text{ cm}^3$

Example 7.2

A spherical ball has a volume of 10.5 cm³. What is its surface area? Give your answer to 1 decimal place.

Solution

$\frac{4}{3}\pi r^3 = \frac{4\pi r^3}{3} = 10.5$

$4\pi r^3 = 31.5$

$r^3 = 2.507$

$r = 1.358 \text{ cm}$

Surface area $= 4\pi r^2 = 23.2 \text{ cm}^2$

Did you remember to write your answer correct to 1 decimal place?

Frustum of a cone

To find the dimensions of a frustum of a cone, take a cross-section of the cone through its axis, and extend the lines to make an isosceles triangle, and halve this to give a right-angled triangle. Use similar figures to find the dimension you need to find.

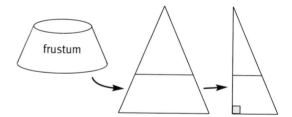

frustum

Example 7.3

The frustum of a cone has a height of 15 cm. If the radii of the top and bottom are 20 cm and 30 respectively, find its volume. Write your answer in terms of π.

Solution

The cross section of the cone is given below: extend the line up to make an isosceles triangle, then halve it to give a right-angled triangle.

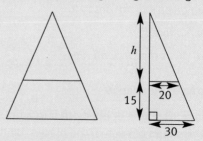

h

15

20

30

Label the height of the missing part of the cone as h.

Using similar figures,

$$\frac{h}{20} = \frac{h+15}{30}$$

$$30h = 20(h+15)$$

 Hints & Tips

Remember to write the h + 15 in brackets!

$$30h = 20h + 300$$
$$10h = 300$$
$$h = 30$$

The frustum is the remainder when a small cone is cut away from the top of a large cone. The base radius and height of the large cone are 30 cm and 45 cm respectively, for the smaller cone they are 20 cm and 30 cm respectively.

Using the formula for the volume of a cone,

$$V = \frac{1}{3}\pi r^2 h$$

$$V = \frac{1}{3}\pi \times 30^2 \times 45 - \frac{1}{3}\pi \times 20^2 \times 30 = 9500\pi \, \text{cm}^3$$

Exercise 7.1

1. Find the volume of the frustum of a cone, with radii 6 cm and 8 cm and height of 12 cm. Leave your answer in terms of π.

2. An object is made from a hollow hemisphere and a cone, like the toy shown in Example 7.1. The cone has a height of 9.1 m and a radius of 8.8 m.
   a) Find the volume of the entire object.
   b) The object stands on its hemispherical base, with the height of the cone vertical, and is then filled with sand up to a height of 10.3 m from the base of the hemisphere. Find the volume of sand contained in the object.

3. A solid cone has a base radius of 6 cm and a height of 8 cm. Find its surface area.

Answers 7.1

1. $\dfrac{h+12}{h} = \dfrac{8}{6} \Rightarrow h = 36$

   $V = \frac{1}{3}\pi \times 8^2 \times 48 - \frac{1}{3}\pi \times 6^2 \times 36 = 592\pi \, \text{cm}^2$

2. a) Volume of hemisphere $= \frac{2}{3}\pi r^3 = 1427 \, \text{m}^3$

   Volume of cone $= \frac{1}{3}\pi r^2 h = 738 \, \text{m}^3$

   Total volume $= 2165 \, \text{m}^3$

   b) Height of sand in the cone
   $= 10.3 - 8.8 = 1.5 \, \text{m}$

   So the unfilled height of the cone is
   $9.1 - 1.5 = 7.6 \, \text{m}$

   Using similar triangles, the radius of the unfilled part is $\frac{7.6}{9.1} \times 8.8 = 7.35 \, \text{m}$

   Volume of unfilled part of the cone
   $= \frac{1}{3}\pi r^2 h = 430 \, \text{m}^3$

   So total volume of sand
   $= 2165 - 430 = 1735 \, \text{m}^3$

3. Slant height $l = \sqrt{6^2 + 8^2} = 10$

   Curved surface area $= \pi \times 6 \times 10 = 188.5 \, \text{cm}^2$

   Base area $= 113.1 \, \text{cm}^2$

   Total surface area $= 302 \, \text{cm}^2$

Dimensions

In questions on dimensions you will be given expressions and asked whether they relate to length, area or volume, or are impossibilities.

These questions are easier to understand if you work in a basic unit. For convenience, we shall use cm, cm² or cm³ in the following way.

Length	cm	1 dimension
Area	cm²	2 dimensions
Volume	cm³	3 dimensions

Note: Any measurement of length, area or volume follows the same pattern.

Rule 1 – adding (or subtracting) like with like

- length + length = length (or perimeter)
  cm + cm = cm

- area + area = area
  cm² + cm² = cm²

- volume + volume = volume
  cm³ + cm³ = cm³

Rule 2 – multiplication of dimensions

Use TIP (Times ⇒ Indices Plus)

- length × length = area
  cm¹ × cm¹ = cm²

- length × length × length = volume
  cm¹ × cm¹ × cm¹ = cm³

- area × length = volume
  cm² × cm¹ = cm³

Rule 3 – division of dimensions

Use DIM (Divide ⇒ Indices Minus)

- volume ÷ area = length
  $cm^3 \div cm^2 = cm^1$
- volume ÷ length = area
  $cm^3 \div cm^1 = cm^2$

Rule 4 – adding or subtracting different dimensions gives a nonsense result

For example   length + area = nonsense!
                   volume + area = nonsense!

If possible work with the expressions alone. The diagrams are often confusing and unnecessary.

Follow this infallible method.

1 Cross out all the whole numbers, fractions and πs (but do not cross out the indices).
2 Each remaining letter represents a dimension. Change each of them to cm^1, cm^2 or cm^3 as appropriate.
3 Simplify the expression, following the four rules.
4 Look at your final answer and decide whether it represents length, area, volume or none of these.

Example 7.4

The letters p, q and r represent lengths. Are the following formulae for length, area, volume or none of these?

a) $\pi p^2 q - 2r^2$ **b)** $\frac{4}{3}\pi pqr$ **c)** $p\sqrt{q^2 - r^2}$

d) $\pi p(2q + r)$ **e)** $\frac{4p^3}{qr}$

Solution

Step 1: Cross out all numbers (this includes π and fractions).

a) $\pi p^2 q - 2r^2$ **b)** $\frac{4}{3}\pi pqr$ **c)** $p\sqrt{q^2 - r^2}$

d) $\pi p(2q + r)$ **e)** $\frac{4p^3}{qr}$

Steps 2 to 4: Convert all lengths to cm, areas to cm^2 and volumes to cm^3, and combine them.

a) $p^2 q - r^2 = cm^2 cm - cm^2 = cm^3 - cm^2$
     = none of these!

b) $pqr = cm \times cm \times cm = cm^3$ = volume

c) $p\sqrt{q^2 - r^2} = cm\sqrt{cm^2 - cm^2} = cm\sqrt{cm^2}$
     $= cm \times cm = cm^2$ = area

d) $p(q + r) = cm(cm + cm) = cm \times cm = cm^2$
     = area

e) $\frac{p^3}{qr} = cm^3 \div cm^2 = cm$ = length

Exercise 7.2

The letters p, q and r represent lengths. Decide whether the following are lengths, areas, volumes, or none of these.

1 $4\pi r^2 + r\sqrt{p^2 + q^2}$ **2** $\frac{2p^2}{\pi r}$ **3** $6pr^2 - \pi q^2 r$

4 $2pq + 3r$ **5** $\sqrt{p^2 + q^2 + qr}$ **6** $\frac{\pi pq^2}{6r}$

Answers 7.2

1 area	**2** length	**3** volume
4 none of these		
5 length	**6** area	

 **TAKE A BREAK**

Take a break and take stock, before you go on to scale factors.

Length, area and volume scale factors for similar figures

 If two figures are similar, one is an exact enlargement of the other. The word 'enlargement' can also be applied to shapes becoming smaller.

To calculate the volume scale factor when you have an area scale factor (and vice versa), you need to find the length scale factor first.

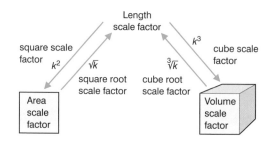

If one object has length 2 times as big as another, then the area will be 2^2 times as big and the volume 2^3 times as big.

If one object has length k times as big as another, then the area will be k^2 times as big and the volume k^3 times as big.

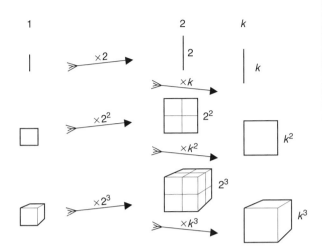

Similar shapes

If the areas are in the ratio $k : 1$, then the lengths are in the ratio $\sqrt{k} : 1$ (or $k^{\frac{1}{2}} : 1$).

If the volumes are in the ratio $k : 1$, then the lengths are in the ratio $\sqrt[3]{k} : 1$ (or $k^{\frac{1}{3}} : 1$).

Example 7.5

The Dog and Duck sells home-brewed beer in similar bottles. The height of the smaller bottle is 15 cm and the height of the larger bottle is 30 cm. If the smaller bottle holds 0.75 litres, how much does the larger hold?

Solution

Step 1: Firstly find the length scale factor.
Second **O**ver **F**irs**T** = $30 \div 15 = 2$

Step 2: Volume scale factor = $k^3 = 2^3 = 8$

So the larger bottle holds 8 times as much as the smaller bottle.

Volume = $8 \times 0.75 = 6$ litres

Example 7.6

Two tents are put up on a camp site. One tent has dimensions 2.5 times those of the other tent. If the smaller tent has a base area of $16\,\text{m}^2$ and a volume of $45\,\text{m}^3$, evaluate the area and volume of the larger tent.

Solution

Area = $2.5^2 \times 16 = 100\,\text{m}^2$
Volume = $2.5^3 \times 45 = 703\,\text{m}^3$

Example 7.7

A third tent is put up on the camp site of Example 7.6. It is similar to the larger tent but has lengths 0.8 of the lengths of the larger tent. Work out the area and volume of the new tent.

Solution

Area = $0.8^2 \times 100 = 64\,\text{m}^2$

Volume = $0.8^3 \times 703 = 360\,\text{m}^3$

Example 7.8

Two cylinders are similar. The surface area of the larger cylinder is $296.45\,\text{m}^2$ and the surface area of the smaller cylinder is $24.2\,\text{m}^2$.

a) Find the area scale factor of the enlargement from the larger to the smaller cylinder.

b) If the height of the larger cylinder is $26.25\,\text{m}$, find the height of the smaller cylinder.

Solution

a)   Area scale factor = $24.2 \div 296.45 = 0.0816$

b)   Length scale factor = $\sqrt{0.0816} = 0.286$

Height = $26.25 \times \sqrt{0.0816} = 7.5\,\text{m}$

Example 7.9

A florist's shop has similar windows in the office and the shop front. The areas of the windows are $1.4\,\text{m}^2$ and $8.75\,\text{m}^2$ respectively. If the length of the office window is 80 cm, what would be the corresponding length of the shop window?

Solution

Area scale factor = $8.75 \div 1.4 = 6.25$

Length = $0.80 \times \sqrt{6.25} = 2\,\text{m}$

Example 7.10

Two similar oil cans hold 6 litres and 2.2 litres. If the larger one is 35 cm high, find the height of the smaller one.

Solution

Volume scale factor = $2.2 \div 6 = 0.367$

Length scale factor = $\sqrt[3]{0.367} = 0.716$

Height of can = $35 \times 0.716 = 25.1$ cm

Length, area and volume

Exercise 7.3

1 Two flagpoles are similar, the larger being 1.75 times the height of the smaller.

   a) If the smaller flagpole is 8.5 m high, find the height of the larger flagpole.

   b) If the smaller pole uses 6.7 m³ of wood, find the volume the larger pole.

2 A school secretary's office has a length and width 3.7 times those of the waiting room next door. If the area of the waiting room is 10.1 m², find the area of the secretary's office.

3 A type of biscuit is sold in two similar packets. Large packets are 24 cm long and small packets are 15 cm long. If large packets weigh 450 g, find how much the smaller packet weighs, to the nearest gram.

4 Nina ordered a rectangular poster of area 600 cm², to advertise the end-of-term concert. When the poster arrived, it was found to be similar but of area 864 cm².

   a) What was the area scale factor?

   b) What was the linear scale factor?

   c) If the length ordered was 30 cm, what was the length of the poster delivered?

5 A winery keeps its red wine in a large barrel holding 600 litres. It is sold to customers in similar barrels which hold 5 litres. If the height of the large barrel is 1.6 m, find the height of the smaller barrel.

Answers 7.3

(answers printed upside-down)

5 0.32 m or 32 cm

4 a) 1.44   **b)** 1.2   **c)** 36 cm

2 138.3 m²   **3** 110 g

1 a) 14.9 m **b)** 35.9 m³

TAKE A BREAK

Take another break.

Exam-type questions 7

1 a, b and c are lengths. State whether each of the following formulae represents a length, area, volume or none of these.

   a) $\frac{1}{4}\pi a^2 b + b^3$ **b)** $\pi a b - \frac{3}{4}b^3$

   c) $\sqrt{b^2 + c^2}$ **d)** $b^3 \div a$

   e) $a(b^2 + \pi c^2)$ **f)** $\frac{\pi a^2 b}{c^2}$

2 A scoop, illustrated below, is in the form of a prism. The shaded end is a trapezium. Find the volume of the scoop.

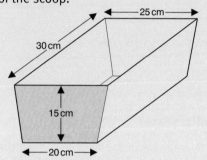

3 The diagram represents a flower bed.

   a) Find its perimeter.

   b) Find its area.

   c) If it is covered by compost to a depth of 15 cm, give the volume of compost in cubic metres.

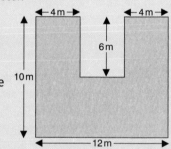

4 A cylindrical glass, full of water, has volume 186.5 cm³. If its diameter is 5 cm, how deep is the water?

5 State, with a reason, whether the following pairs of triangles are definitely congruent.

   a)

   b)

   c)

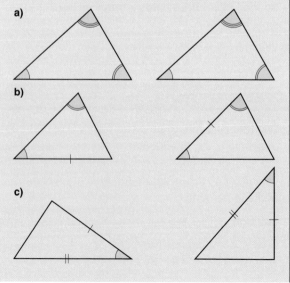

6 Two containers are similar. The areas of their bases are 5.3 m² and 33.125 m². If the height of the smaller is 4.8 m find the height of the larger.

7 Two triangular-based prisms are similar. The smaller has a volume of 648 cm³ and a cross-sectional area of 54 cm². If the volume of the larger prism is 17 496 cm³, find the length of the larger.

8 A map is drawn to the scale of 1 : 25 000. A field has an area on the map of 6 cm². What is its actual area, in km²?

9 Two triangles are similar. The area of triangle A is 4 cm² and the area of triangle B is 9 cm². Write the ratio of areas in the form A : B, and that of their sides in the same form.

10 A cuboid with a volume 2.475 litres is filled with water. The contents are poured into a cylinder of radius 6 cm.

   a) What would be the depth of the water in the cylinder?

   b) The contents are then poured into a second cylindrical vessel, filling it completely. If the height of this vessel is 18.2 cm, find the base radius.

11 The area of a plate is 16.5 cm². Find its diameter.

12 A model of a boat is built to a scale of 1 : 60. If the real boat is 17.2 m long, find the length of the model in centimetres, correct to one decimal place.

13 A regular square-based pyramid has a base length of 5.6 cm and a vertical height of 6.7 cm. Find:

   a) the angle between a triangular face and the square base

   b) the angle between an edge and the square base

   c) the length of an edge from the top of the pyramid to a base vertex.

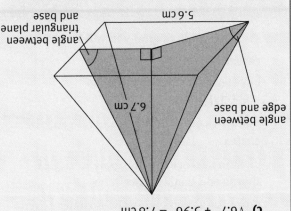

13 a) $\tan^{-1}(6.7 \div 2.8) = 67°$

   b) Diagonal of square base $= \sqrt{5.6^2 + 5.6^2}$
      $= 7.92$ cm
      Half of diagonal $= 3.96$ cm
      Angle $= \tan^{-1}(6.7 \div 3.96) = 59°$

   c) $\sqrt{6.7^2 + 3.96^2} = 7.8$ cm

12 28.7 cm

11 diameter $= 4.6$ cm (remember 2r)

10 a) 21.9 cm   **b)** 6.6 cm

9 Area 4 : 9 or 1 : 2.25, sides 2 : 3 or 1 : 1.5

   3 750 000 000 cm² = 375 000 m² = 0.375 km²

   field area $= 6 \times 625 000 000 =$
   $= 625 000 000$

8 length $= 1 : 25 000$, area $= 1^2 : 25 000^2 =$
   1 : 625 000 000

7 17 496 ÷ 648 $= 27 =$ volume scale factor;
   $\sqrt[3]{27} = 3$; 648 ÷ 54 $= 12$ (length of smaller prism); length of larger prism $= 12 \times 3 = 36$ cm

6 12 m   33.125 ÷ 5.3 $= 6.25 =$ area scale factor; length scale factor $= \sqrt{6.25} = 2.5$

5 a) similar, not necessarily congruent as no lengths are given
   b) not necessarily congruent as the given sides do not correspond   **c)** congruent (SAS)

REVIEW

How much have you learnt?
Tick off each topic in the list when you are confident that you can cope with it.

☐ Calculate the area of a triangle.

☐ Calculate the area and circumference of a circle.

☐ Find the volume and surface area of 3D shapes, including the frustum of a cone.

☐ Identify the dimensions in an expression and check that the quantity is valid.

☐ Calculate scale factors for area and volume, given a linear scale factor for similar shapes.

Answers

4 9.5 cm

3 a) 56 m   **b)** 96 m²
   c) 14.4 m³ (15 cm = 0.15 m)

2 volume $= 10 125$ cm³

1 a) volume **b)** none **c)** length **d)** area
   e) volume **f)** length

Circle theorems

You need to learn nine basic rules about circles. These can be classified into three different sections, which are:

- angles
- chords
- tangents.

You will often be asked to give reasons for your answer, so make sure that you memorise the description for each rule. You also need to know what a cyclic quadrilateral is – it just means that all four vertices lie on the circumference of the same circle.

Angles: four rules

1 The angle subtended at the circumference by the diameter of a circle is 90°.

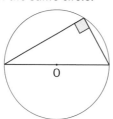

2 The angle subtended at the centre of a circle is twice the angle subtended at the circumference from the same two points.

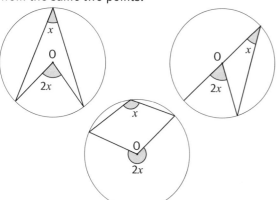

3 The angles subtended anywhere at the circumference from the same two points are equal.

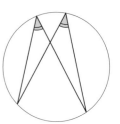

4 Opposite angles of a cyclic quadrilateral add up to 180°. (Conversely, if opposite angles of a quadrilateral add up to 180°, the vertices lie on the circumference of a circle.)

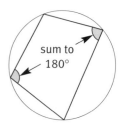

Chords: two rules

5 The perpendicular bisector of a chord passes through the centre of the circle.

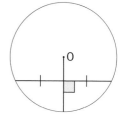

6 If the radius passes through the midpoint of a chord, then the two lines are perpendicular and two congruent triangles are formed.

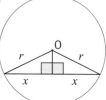

Tangents: three rules

7 The angle between a tangent and the radius at the point of contact is 90°.

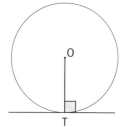

8 Tangents from a common point are equal in length.

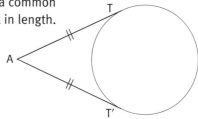

9 The alternate segment theorem – the angle between a tangent and a chord at the point of contact is equal to the angle subtended by that chord in the alternate segment.

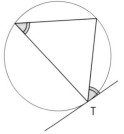

Now you can **ACT** on circles: **A**ngles, **C**hords, **T**angents.

Example 8.1

The line POR is the diameter of the circle, centre O. Giving a reason for your answer, find the size of the following angles:

a) QPR

b) QSR

c) SOR

d) ORS

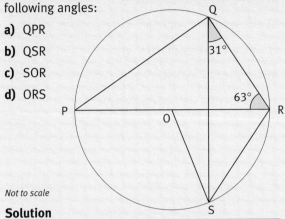

Not to scale

Solution

a) 27°. The angle PQR is 90° because line POR is the diameter. ($\angle$QPR = 180° − (90° + 63°))

b) 27°. It is the same as angle QPR because they are subtended from common points (Q and R).

c) 62°. The angle at the centre is twice the angle at the circumference (SQR).

d) 59°. Triangle ORS is isosceles, because OR and OS are radii.

Example 8.2

The lines AB and AD are tangents to the circle, centre O. Find the size of the following angles, giving reasons for your answer:

a) BAD   b) BDO

c) BOD   d) BCD

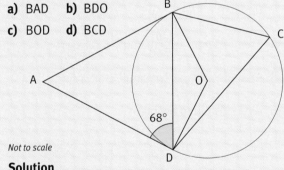

Not to scale

Solution

a) 44°. Triangle ABD is isosceles because tangents from a common point are equal.

b) 22°. $\angle$ODA = 90° (angle between tangent and radius) $\angle$BDO = 90° − 68° = 22°

c) 136°. Triangle BOD is isosceles (OB and OD are radii).

d) 68°. Either because it is half the angle at the origin (136°) or it is the same as angle ADB because of the alternate segment theorem.

Proof of circle theorems

You may be asked to prove one of the circle theorems. Two examples are given here. For more, refer to your teacher or a textbook.

Example 8.3

Prove the alternate segment theorem.

Solution

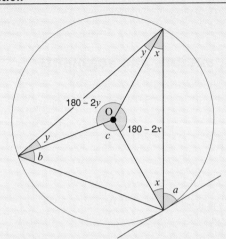

Draw a diagram: connect the vertices of the cyclic triangle to the centre of the circle to form three isosceles triangles. Label the angles as shown.

The angle between a tangent and its radius is 90°, so $a + x = 90$.

Angles at the centre of the circle sum to 360°:

$c = 360 − (180 − 2x + 180 − 2y)$

$c = 2x + 2y$

$b = \dfrac{180 − (2x + 2y)}{2}$

$\quad = 90 − x − y$

$\therefore b + y = 90 − x$

From above, we have $a = 90 − x$

$\therefore a = b + y$

Example 8.4

Prove that the angle subtended from two points on the circumference at the origin is twice the angle at the circumference.

Solution

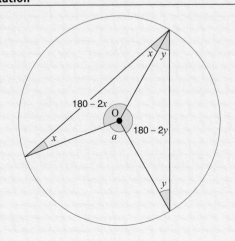

Draw a diagram: divide the quadrilateral into two isosceles triangles and label the angles as shown.

$$a = 360 - (180 - 2x + 180 - 2y)$$
$$= 2x + 2y$$
$$= 2(x + y)$$

Arcs, sectors and segments

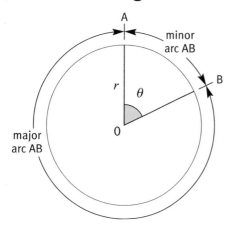

Length of arc $= \dfrac{\theta}{360} \times 2\pi r$

or $\dfrac{\theta}{360} \times \pi d$

Area of sector $= \dfrac{\theta}{360} \times \pi r^2$

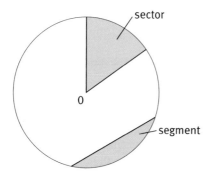

Area of any triangle ABC $= \dfrac{1}{2}ab \sin C$

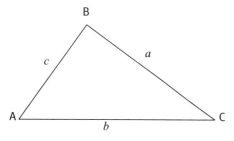

Area of segment = area of sector − area of triangle

Example 8.5

In the circle below, find:

a) the length of minor arc XY

b) the length of major arc XY

c) the area of sector OXY

d) the area of △OXY

e) the area of the shaded segment.

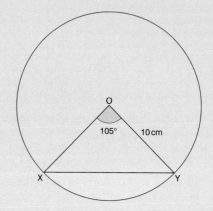

Solution

a) Arc length $= \dfrac{\theta}{360} \times 2\pi r = 18.3$ cm

b) Major arc XY (this is the long way round from

X to Y) $= \dfrac{\theta}{360} \times 2\pi r = 44.5$ cm

(using $\theta = 360° - 105° = 255°$)

c) Area of sector $= \dfrac{\theta}{360} \times \pi r^2 = 91.6$ cm^2

d) Area of △OXY $= \dfrac{1}{2}ab\sin C = 48.3$ cm^2

e) Area of shaded segment
$= 91.6 - 48.3 = 43.3$ cm^2

 TAKE A BREAK

Mind in a spin? Take a break and prepare for the exam-type questions.

Exam-type questions 8

1 JL and KL are tangents to the circle centred at O. M is a point on the circumference of this circle. Find the angles *a*, *b* and *c*.

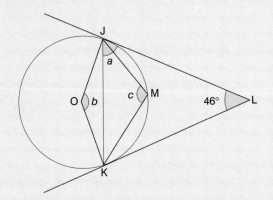

2 DE is a chord of a circle centred at C, with a radius of 7.5 cm. Angle DCE = 124°.

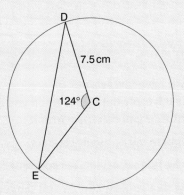

Find:
a) the area of the sector CDE
b) the area of triangle CDE
c) the area of the shaded segment.

3 PR passes through O, the centre of the circle. Angle PRQ = 55° and angle PQS = 25°. Find:
a) angle QSR   b) angle POS   c) angle OSR.

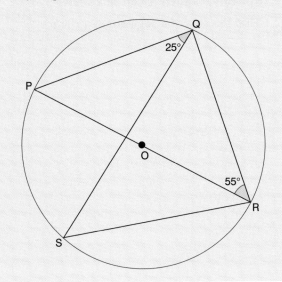

4 ABC is a sector of a circle centred at A, and with radius 18.4 mm. Find:
a) the length of the minor arc BC
b) the area of the sector.

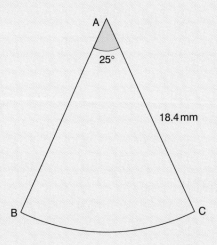

5 AB is a tangent to a circle with centre O, and C, D, E and F are points on the circumference such that angle OCE = 28°. Find angles *x* and *y*, giving reasons for your answers.

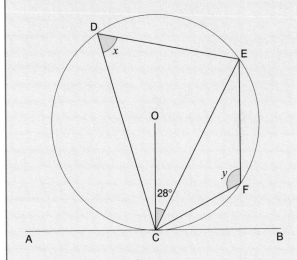

6 ABCE is a rectangle. AB = 5 cm and AE = 6 cm. CED is a quadrant of a circle centred at E. Find:
a) the perimeter of the shape
b) the area.

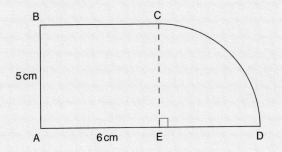

7 HJKL is a rectangle and HJ is a chord of a circle centred at M.

   a) Using the cosine rule, find the angle HMJ.

   b) Find the area of the sector HMJ.

   c) Find the area of triangle HMJ.

   d) Hence or otherwise, find the area of the whole shape.

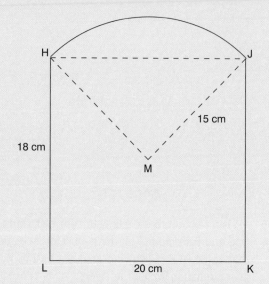

8 DEF is a sector of a circle centred at D. If the length of the minor arc EF is 4 cm, find θ to the nearest degree.

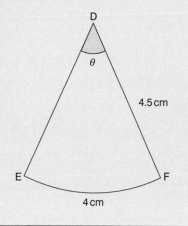

R E V I E W

How much have you learnt?
Tick off each topic in the list when you are confident that you can cope with it.

☐ **Recognise cyclic quadrilaterals.**

☐ **Use the rules applying to cyclic quadrilaterals.**

☐ **Recognise angles, chords and tangents in circles.**

☐ **Use the basic rules that apply to angles, chords and tangents in circles.**

☐ **Prove the various rules about circles (circle theorems).**

☐ **Find the area of a sector of a circle.**

☐ **Find the length of an arc of a circle.**

☐ **Find the area of a segment of a circle.**

By the end of this chapter you will be able to:

- recognise the transformations: reflection, rotation, enlargement and translation

- find the scale factor of an enlargement

- recognise vector quantities

- combine two vectors by drawing triangles and using trigonometry

- solve problems involving practical applications of vectors.

Transformations in the plane

The numbers next to each type of transformation below show how many extra points you can pick up by including all the relevant pieces of information.

Below are the four types of transformations you need to know, and the information which fully describes them:

Reflections 1: line of reflection.

Rotations 3: centre, direction, angle of rotation.

Translations 1: vector.

Enlargements 2: centre, scale factor.

Reflections

Any point on an object, when reflected in a line, ends up equidistant from the line; and the line joining the points is perpendicular to the line of reflection.

Rotations

Most rotations will be of 180° (in which case you do not need to state the direction of the rotation) or 90°.

If you need to find the centre of rotation of an object and its image, connect a point on the object with its point on the image. Draw the perpendicular bisector of this line. Repeat for another pair of points. The centre of rotation is the point where the two perpendicular bisectors meet.

Translations

A translation of $\begin{pmatrix} 2 \\ -5 \end{pmatrix}$ moves the object +2 in the x-direction and −5 in the y-direction.

Enlargements

To find the scale factor (s.f.) of an enlargement, use **S**econd **O**ver **F**irs**T** (**SOFT**)

You need the ratio of the image length to the original length.

$$\text{scale factor} = \frac{\text{image length}}{\text{original length}}$$

Compare this with scale factors in Chapter 7, Length, area and volume.

If the scale factor is between −1 and 1, the 'enlargement' will in fact be smaller than the original.

To find the centre of an enlargement, connect related points on the object and image and then extend them. The centre of enlargement is the point where these lines cross. An enlargement makes the object smaller when the scale factor is between −1 and 1 (i.e. −1<s.f.<1). A negative scale factor means the image is on the opposite side of the centre of the enlargement. To find the scale factor of an enlargement, take any length on the image and divide by the related length on the original object.

In the diagram below, the image of P after an enlargement with scale factor $\frac{1}{2}$, centre O, is Q and the image of P after enlargement with factor $-\frac{1}{2}$, centre O, is R.

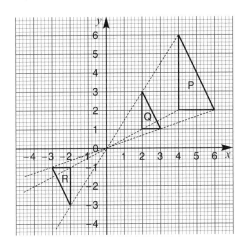

Example 9.1

1 Carry out the transformations listed below.

a) Reflect the triangle labelled A in the y-axis. Label the reflection B.

b) Reflect triangle A in the line $y = -x$. Label the reflection C.

c) Rotate triangle A 90° clockwise, centred at (0, 0). Label the triangle D.

d) Enlarge triangle A by a scale factor $\frac{1}{2}$, centre (0, 0). Label the enlargement E.

e) Translate triangle A by a vector of $\binom{3}{-1}$. Label the translation F.

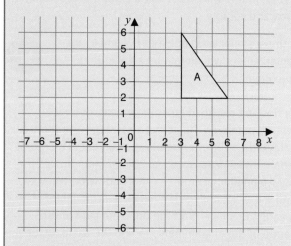

2 What single transformation would map B to D?

3 Describe fully the transformation which maps B to C.

Solution

1

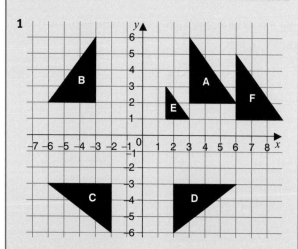

2 Reflection in $y = x$.

3 Anti-clockwise rotation 90°, centred at (0, 0).

Example 9.2

Describe the transformation from ABC to A'B'C'.

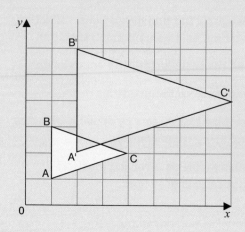

Solution

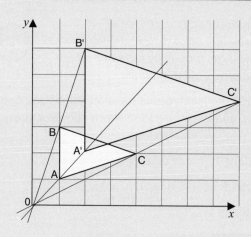

A'B'C' is an enlargement of ABC, scale factor 2, centred on (0, 0).

Example 9.3

On the diagram below, transform triangle T through a rotation of 90° clockwise, centred at (0, 0).

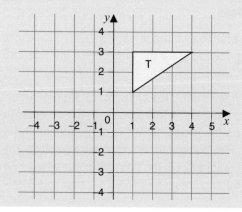

Solution

The triangle would move into the quadrant which is immediately below it.

Turn the page round so that the required quadrant is now at the top right-hand corner.

Now imagine your original triangle in exactly the same place as it was before.

Alternatively, use tracing paper to trace the object. Hold your pencil firmly, with its point at the origin, and keep it there as you rotate the tracing paper through 90° clockwise.

Try looking at each original point and work out its new coordinates using left and right, and up and down.

Hints & Tips

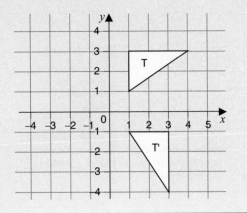

Vectors

Vectors represent movement. Vectors are written in columns, with the horizontal component (the movement in the x-direction) above the vertical component (the movement in the y-direction).

Always follow the direction of the arrow.

Remember that you can also go in the negative direction.

Vector notation can be confusing!

- $\overrightarrow{OA}$ may also be written as $\mathbf{a}$ or $-\overrightarrow{AO}$
- $\overrightarrow{AO}$ is the same as $-\mathbf{a}$ or $-\overrightarrow{OA}$
- $\overrightarrow{AB} = \overrightarrow{AO} + \overrightarrow{OB} = -\overrightarrow{OA} + \overrightarrow{OB} = -\mathbf{a} + \mathbf{b} = \mathbf{b} - \mathbf{a}$

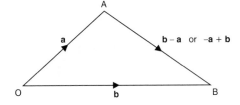

A vector has **magnitude** (i.e. size) and **direction**.

The magnitude of a vector is represented by its length. You can find this by using Pythagoras' theorem.

For example, the magnitude of $\begin{pmatrix} -2 \\ 3 \end{pmatrix}$ is $\sqrt{2^2 + 3^2} = 3.6$.

The direction of a vector is the angle that the vector makes with a given direction.

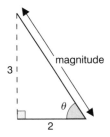

For example, the direction of $\begin{pmatrix} -2 \\ 3 \end{pmatrix}$ is

$\theta = \tan^{-1}(3 \div 2) = 56.3°$ to the negative x-direction.

Two vectors are parallel if one is a multiple of the other. Collinear points are points that are on the same straight line.

Hints & Tips

Example 9.4

In the diagram below, $\overrightarrow{OB} = \mathbf{x}$, $\overrightarrow{OD} = \mathbf{y}$ and $\overrightarrow{OA} = \overrightarrow{DC}$.

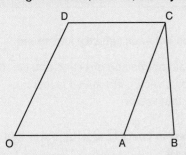

a) If $\overrightarrow{DC} = \frac{2}{3}\overrightarrow{OB}$, find $\overrightarrow{DC}$ in terms of $\mathbf{x}$ and $\mathbf{y}$.

b) Find $\overrightarrow{CA}$.

c) Is OACD a parallelogram? Justify your answer.

d) Give $\overrightarrow{CB}$ in terms of $\mathbf{x}$ and $\mathbf{y}$.

Solution

a) $\overrightarrow{DC} = \frac{2}{3}\mathbf{x}$ or $\frac{2\mathbf{x}}{3}$

b) $\overrightarrow{CA} = \overrightarrow{CD} + \overrightarrow{DO} + \overrightarrow{OA} = -\frac{2}{3}\mathbf{x} - \mathbf{y} + \frac{2}{3}\mathbf{x} = -\mathbf{y}$

c) OACD is a parallelogram because both pairs of opposite sides are parallel and equal in length.

d) $\overrightarrow{CB} = \overrightarrow{CD} + \overrightarrow{DO} + \overrightarrow{OB} = -\frac{2}{3}\mathbf{x} - \mathbf{y} + \mathbf{x} = \frac{1}{3}\mathbf{x} - \mathbf{y}$

Transformations

Exercise 9.1

In the diagram $\overrightarrow{OA} = \textbf{a}$ and $\overrightarrow{OB} = \textbf{b}$. OACB is a parallelogram. B is the midpoint of $\overrightarrow{CD}$ and E is the midpoint of $\overrightarrow{OB}$.

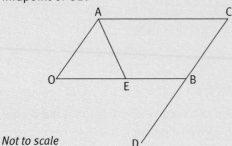

Not to scale

Find, in terms of **a** and **b**, the vectors:

a) $\overrightarrow{OC}$

b) $\overrightarrow{AE}$

c) $\overrightarrow{AD}$

d) Are points A, E and D collinear? Give a reason for your answer.

Answers 9.1

a) $\textbf{a} + \textbf{b}$

b) $-\textbf{a} + \frac{1}{2}\textbf{b}$ or $\frac{1}{2}\textbf{b} - \textbf{a}$

c) $-2\textbf{a} + \textbf{b}$ or $\textbf{b} - 2\textbf{a}$

d) Yes, they are collinear (i.e. they lie in a straight line) because $\overrightarrow{AD}$ is a multiple of $\overrightarrow{AE}$. ($\overrightarrow{AD} = 2\overrightarrow{AE}$)

The difference between velocity and speed

Velocity has magnitude and direction and can be represented by a vector, but speed is just the magnitude of that vector.

Vectors applied to boats in moving water and planes in the air

In these questions, you have to construct a right-angled triangle. You need to consider:

- the direction in which the craft would be going if there were no current or wind

- the air or water current

- the resultant direction (the direction in which the craft is actually going).

Draw all the velocities on one right-angled triangle, and all the distances on another.

Hints & Tips

When drawing the velocities, start by drawing a line for the direction in which the craft would be moving if the water were still. At the end of this line, draw the direction of the current. Join the free ends of these two lines to make a right-angled triangle. The third length is the resultant velocity. It usually helps to make the velocity triangle smaller than the distance triangle. These two triangles will be similar.

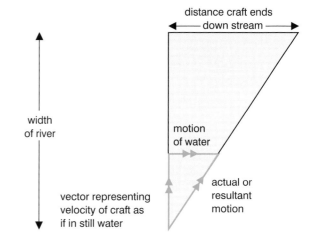

OR

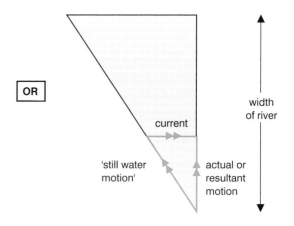

Most questions can be solved using X-Direct, trigonometry, Pythagoras' theorem or the STV triplet.

Example 9.5

After a practice session with the canoeing club, Ranjit finds himself on the wrong side of the river. He can paddle his canoe at 0.6 m/s in still water. The river runs at right angles to the bank at a speed of 0.35 m/s. He needs to cross from point A to B, the nearest point on the opposite bank.

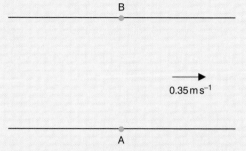

a) Find, by calculation, the direction to AB in which he must head initially.
b) Calculate his resultant speed in the direction AB.
c) If the river is 200 m wide, how long does it take him to cross? Give your answer to the nearest 10 seconds.
d) If he aims the boat continually in a direction perpendicular to the flow of the water, how far downstream from B will he land?

Solution

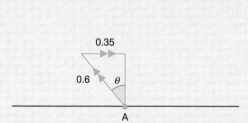

a) $\sin^{-1}(0.35 \div 0.6) = 35.7°$
b) $\sqrt{0.6^2 - 0.35^2} = 0.49$ m/s
c) Using the STV triplet:
$$\text{time} = \frac{200}{0.49} = 410 \text{ seconds}$$

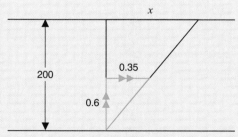

d) Speed   Distance
0.6   200
0.35

$$\text{Distance} = \frac{0.35 \times 200}{0.6} = 117 \text{ m}$$

Exercise 9.2

1 The current of the river runs parallel to its straight banks at a speed of 0.25 m/s. A boat, capable of travelling at 0.65 m/s in still water, crosses the river.

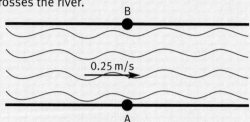

a) i) In which direction must the boat head in order to end up on the other bank at point B, directly opposite point A?
   ii) What is its resultant speed?
  iii) If the river is of width 60 m, how long will it take to cross?
b) A second boat, also capable of travelling at 0.65 m/s in still water, crosses from A. It moves so that it is constantly facing in a direction perpendicular to the direction of the current.
   i) What is its resultant speed?
   ii) What is its resultant direction?
  iii) How far downstream from B will the boat land on the opposite bank?
   iv) How long does it take to cross?

2

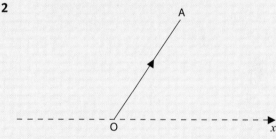

If the vector $\overrightarrow{OA} = \begin{pmatrix} 5 \\ 12 \end{pmatrix}$, find:
a) its magnitude
b) the angle it makes with the x-axis.

3 In the triangle OAB, P is the midpoint of OA, and Q is the midpoint of OB.

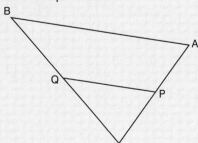

If $\overrightarrow{OA} = \mathbf{a}$ and $\overrightarrow{OB} = \mathbf{b}$, express, in terms of $\mathbf{a}$ and $\mathbf{b}$:
a) $\overrightarrow{AB}$ b) $\overrightarrow{PQ}$ c) $\overrightarrow{AQ}$.
d) Are AB and PQ parallel? Give a reason for your answer.

Answers 9.2

1 a)

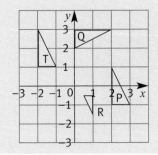

0.25 m/s, resultant, 0.65 m/s

i) $\sin^{-1}(0.25 \div 0.65) = 23°$ from the perpendicular to the bank.

ii) $\sqrt{(0.65^2 - 0.25^2)} = 0.6$ m/s

iii) $60 \div 0.6 = 100$ seconds

b)

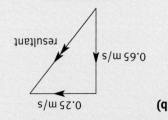

0.25 m/s, resultant, 0.65 m/s

i) $\sqrt{(0.65^2 + 0.25^2)} = 0.70$ m/s

ii) $\tan^{-1}(0.25 \div 0.65) = 21°$ from the perpendicular to the bank

iii) It is easiest to use similar triangles – and X-Direct – here.

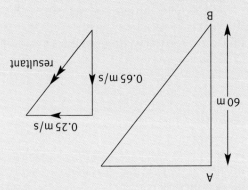

A, 60 m, B, 0.25 m/s, 0.65 m/s, resultant

Speed (m/s)	Distance (m)
0.65	60
0.25	0.65

$\text{Distance} = \dfrac{0.25 \times 60}{0.65} = 23$ m

iv) $60 \div 0.65 = 92$ seconds

2 a) 13 **b)** 67.4°

3 a) $\overrightarrow{AB} = \mathbf{b} - \mathbf{a}$ or $-\mathbf{a} + \mathbf{b}$

b) As $\overrightarrow{OP} = \frac{1}{2}\mathbf{a}$ and $\overrightarrow{OQ} = \frac{1}{2}\mathbf{b}$, $\overrightarrow{PQ} = \frac{1}{2}(\mathbf{b} - \mathbf{a})$

c) $\overrightarrow{AQ} = -\mathbf{a} + \frac{1}{2}\mathbf{b}$ **d)** Yes, because $\overrightarrow{PQ} = \frac{1}{2}\overrightarrow{AB}$

STOP **TAKE A BREAK**

Exam-type questions 9

1 In the diagram, what single transformation maps:
a) P on to Q
b) Q on to R
c) P on to R?

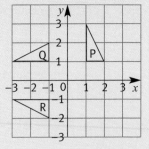

2 In the regular hexagon below, $\overrightarrow{OP} = \mathbf{p}$ and $\overrightarrow{OQ} = \mathbf{q}$. Express the following in terms of $\mathbf{p}$ and $\mathbf{q}$.
a) $\overrightarrow{QR}$ **b)** $\overrightarrow{OR}$ **c)** $\overrightarrow{UQ}$

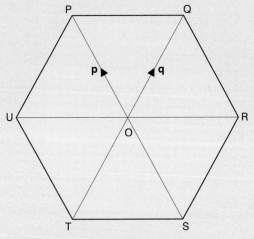

3 A woman can swim at 0.3 m/s in still water. The current in a river 40 m wide flows at a speed of 0.55 m/s in a direction parallel with the banks. If she always faces in a direction perpendicular to the flow of the current, find:
a) her resultant speed
b) the direction from the bank in which she travels
c) how far downstream she lands.

40 m, 0.55 m/s, 0.3 m/s

4 From the diagram below, what single transformation maps triangle T onto:
a) P **b)** Q **c)** R?

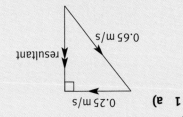

5 An aeroplane can fly at 190 km/h in still air.
   a) If the wind blows in an easterly direction,
       with speed 80 km/h, on what bearing must
       the plane head in order to travel due north?
   b) What will its resultant speed be?

REVIEW

How much have you learnt?
Tick off each topic in the list when you are
confident that you can cope with it.

☐ Recognise the transformations: reflection,
    rotation, enlargement and translation.

☐ Find the scale factor of an enlargement.

☐ Recognise vector quantities.

☐ Combine two vectors by drawing triangles
    and using trigonometry.

☐ Solve problems involving practical
    applications of vectors.

Answers

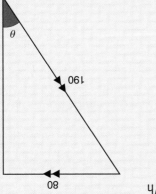

1 a) rotation of 90° anti-clockwise about (0,0)
   b) reflection in the x-axis
   c) reflection in $y = -x$

2 a) $-\mathbf{p}$ b) $\mathbf{q} - \mathbf{p}$ c) $2\mathbf{q} - \mathbf{p}$

3 a) 0.6 m/s   b) 28.6°   c) 73.3 m

4 a) translation $\begin{pmatrix} 4 \\ -2 \end{pmatrix}$
   b) clockwise rotation of 90° centred at (0, 1)
   c) enlargement centred at (0, 0), scale factor $-\frac{1}{2}$

5 a) $\theta = 24.9°$, bearing = 335.1°
   b) 172.3 km/h

Grouped frequency

When you have a large number of values, the data are often given in grouped form.

Here is an example of grouped data. It shows the number of farms in a particular area.

Distance (d) in km from nearest town	Frequency
1 km or less	10
$1 < d \leqslant 2$	15
$2 < d \leqslant 3$	5

$1 < d \leqslant 2$ means a distance between 1 and 2 kilometres, but not including exactly 1 km. A distance of 1 km or less could be written as $0 < d \leqslant 1$ or just $d \leqslant 1$.

Finding the mean from a grouped frequency

In a grouped frequency, you cannot be sure of any exact value, so always use the midpoint of any group.

Example 10.1

In a local survey, 500 citizens were asked how far they lived from their town centre. Their answers were put in this table. Find the mean distance that a citizen lives from the town centre.

Distance (d) between home and town centre (km)	Midpoint (km)	Frequency
1 km or less	0.5	142
$1 < d \leqslant 2$	1.5	108
$2 < d \leqslant 3$	2.5	250

Solution

To find the mean:

*   multiply the frequency by the midpoint
*   add the results
*   divide this total by the total frequency in the usual way.

The mean is
$(0.5 \times 142 + 1.5 \times 108 + 2.5 \times 250) \div 500 = 1.72\,\text{km}$

Make sure that your answer is sensible. If it is obviously wrong, check that you have divided by the total frequency.

By the end of this chapter you will be able to:

*   calculate or evaluate the mean, median and mode of a set of data
*   find the range of a set of data
*   find the quartiles and percentiles of a range of data
*   find the mean from a grouped frequency
*   draw bar charts and histograms
*   find and interpret frequency density
*   draw and interpret pie charts
*   draw a frequency polygon
*   complete a cumulative frequency chart
*   calculate the cumulative frequency for a set of data
*   find the median from a cumulative frequency
*   identify and use the interquartile range
*   draw a box plot
*   calculate moving averages
*   draw and interpret scatter diagrams
*   evaluate sampling methods
*   define data as discrete, continuous, quantitative or qualitative
*   evaluate methods of collecting data.

Averages

The mean, the median and the mode are three ways of expressing the average. This chart summarises how to find the mean, median and mode.

mean	Add together all the values and divide by the number of values you have. (The mean is not necessarily a whole number.)
median	Arrange the values in order of size. The median is the middle value (referred to as the $\frac{1}{2}(n + 1)$ value).
mode	This is the most commonly occurring value. (There can be more than one mode.)

Measures of spread

Range – the difference in value between the largest and smallest values.

Interquartile range – the range of the middle 50% of the data.

Exercise 10.1

The ages in years of the residents of a block of flats are as follows:

Age (a)	Frequency
$0 < a \leqslant 10$	15
$10 < a \leqslant 20$	22
$20 < a \leqslant 30$	30
$30 < a \leqslant 40$	25
$40 < a \leqslant 50$	40
$50 < a \leqslant 80$	23

Find their mean age.

Answers 10.1

Using the midpoints of the groups, their total age is

$$5 \times 15 + 15 \times 22 + 25 \times 30 \times .... = 5325$$

 Note the final group goes from 50 to 80, so the midpoint is 65.

The total number of people is

$$15 + 22 + 30 + ... = 155$$

so their mean age is $5325 \div 155 = 34$ years.

The advantages and disadvantages of using the mean, median and mode

	Advantages	Disadvantages
mean	• most commonly used • easy to calculate	• can be misleading, as if one term is much bigger or much smaller than the others it distorts the mean
median	• often gives a truer picture of the situation • not so affected by extreme values as the mean	• not used very often in the real world • takes longer to calculate because values must first be arranged
mode	• unaffected by extreme values • very appropriate when you need to find the most common result (e.g. if you were a buyer for shoes, you would want to know the most commonly bought sizes.)	• there may be more than one mode • it ignores much of the information

Problems involving the mean

You calculate the mean using the formula

$$\text{mean} = \frac{\text{sum of values}}{\text{number of values}}$$

so:

sum of values = mean × number of values

This second formula is useful when solving more complicated questions on the mean.

Example 10.2

a) Phoebe is representing her class in a school quiz. After five rounds her average score is 24. If she scores 40 in the sixth round, what is her average score after six rounds?

b) In a class of 10 boys and 15 girls, the boys have a mean of 2.4 pets and the girls have a mean of 1.8 pets. Find the mean number of pets of the whole class.

Solution

a) First find her total score after five rounds, i.e. $24 \times 5 = 120$
After six rounds her score is $120 + 40 = 160$
So her new average is $160 \div 6 = 26.7$

b) The boys have a total of $2.4 \times 10 = 24$ pets.
The girls have a total of $1.8 \times 15 = 27$ pets.
The class as a whole has a total of $24 + 27 = 51$ pets.
So the mean number of pets is $51 \div 25 = 2.04$

Exercise 10.2

1. Seven members of a family are sitting in a dinghy which holds 8 people. Their average weight is 84 kg. The dinghy's maximum safe load is 650 kg. What is the most the eighth member could weigh without the dinghy being in danger of sinking?

2. Sam had a total of 45 runs in three games of cricket. If after four games his average number of runs is 14, how many runs did he get in the fourth game?

3. Twelve adults and eight children were asked how many times they had been to the cinema in the last six months. If the mean for the adults was 3.75 and the mean for the children was 6, find the mean for the whole group.

Answers 10.2

So the mean = 93 ÷ 20 = 4.65
The total attendance for the whole group = 93
The total attendance for children = 6 × 8 = 48
= 3.75 × 12 = 45
3 The total attendance for adults
in the fourth game.
= 14 × 4 = 56, so there were 56 − 45 = 11 runs
2 The total runs scored after four games
650 − 588 = 62 kg
the final member must not weigh more than
1 The total weight so far is 84 × 7 = 588 kg, so

Frequency diagrams

Bar charts and histograms

With bar charts, the sample is split up into groups and the height of each bar shows the number of values in the group represented by that bar.

For histograms, the frequency is shown by the area of each bar, not by the height.

The frequency density shows the number of units vertically for every unit horizontally.

For example, a farmer may put 12 cows in each of three different fields of the same area but different dimensions.

If the fields are 2, 6 and 3 furrows wide, the frequency density shows the average number of cows in each furrow.

Remembering Frank FeeDs CoWs gives the triplet relating frequency (F), frequency density (FD) and class width (CW).

$$F = FD \times CW$$
$$FD = \frac{F}{CW} \qquad CW = \frac{F}{FD}$$

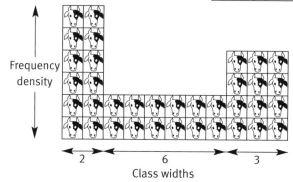

Class widths

Example 10.3

The Tumbleweed Guest House has 95 rooms for guests. The numbers of rooms in the different price ranges are as follows.

Cost (x) per room (£)	Frequency	Class width	Frequency density
$0 < x \leqslant 10$	10		
$10 < x \leqslant 25$	30		
$25 < x \leqslant 40$	45		
$40 < x \leqslant 45$	10		

a) Complete the table.
b) Draw a histogram to represent the data.
c) What does the frequency density represent?

Solution

a)

Cost (x) per room (£)	Frequency	Class width	Frequency density
$0 < x \leqslant 10$	10	10	1
$10 < x \leqslant 25$	30	15	2
$25 < x \leqslant 40$	45	15	3
$40 < x \leqslant 45$	10	5	2

b)

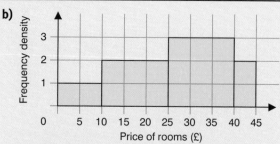

c) The frequency density is the number of rooms per £1 interval.

Exercise 10.3

To celebrate Jenny's 18th birthday, her family, friends and neighbours get together for a party. The people attending are grouped according to age.

Age in years (x)	Frequency	Frequency density (y)
$0 < x \leqslant 10$	100	
$10 < x \leqslant 20$	80	
$20 < x \leqslant 40$	100	
$40 < x \leqslant 55$	15	

1 Complete the table.

2 Complete the histogram.

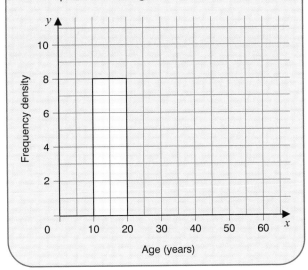

Answers 10.3

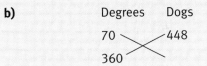

Pie charts

Pie charts are another way of showing frequency. The whole circle (360°) represents the entire sample. Each sector of the pie chart relates to a grouping from the sample.

It may help to use X-Direct.

Example 10.4

A pie chart is used to represent the dogs entered in a dog show. A sector of angle 70° represents the 448 terriers.

a) How many collies were entered if their sector has an angle of 80°?

b) What is the total number of dogs entered in the show?

Solution

a)

	Degrees	Dogs
Terriers	70	448
Collies	80	

Number of collies $= \dfrac{80 \times 448}{70} = 512$

b)

	Degrees	Dogs
	70	448
	360	

Total number of dogs in show

$= \dfrac{360 \times 448}{70} = 2304$

Frequency polygons

These are closely related to bar charts. A frequency polygon is a line on a graph connecting the midpoints of the tops of the bars in order (but the bars themselves are not drawn on a frequency polygon).

Cumulative frequency

To find the cumulative frequency you accumulate (i.e. build up) a running total of the frequencies, starting from the first, until you have included the values of the whole group.

Always write the cumulative frequency on the vertical axis.

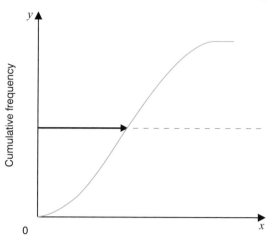

To find the median from a cumulative frequency

As samples usually involve large numbers, you can simply divide the total frequency by 2 to find the position of the median without unduly distorting the result. Then draw a horizontal line to the cumulative frequency graph and draw down to find the median. Leave your lines on the graph.

Lower and upper quartiles

As the word 'quartile' might suggest, these split the sample into quarters. The lower quartile is the item of data 'a quarter of the way up'. The median is the item of data 'halfway up'. The upper quartile is the item 'three-quarters of the way up'. To find the value of:

a) the lower quartile (LQ), divide the total frequency by 4

b) the upper quartile (UQ), multiply the number you found for the LQ by 3 (i.e. it is three-quarters of the sample). Then draw the lines as with the median.

Remember

• When drawing a cumulative frequency graph, plot the graph using the endpoints of the class widths.

• The inter-quartile range is the result of subtracting the lower quartile ($\frac{n}{4}$th value) from the upper quartile ($\frac{3n}{4}$th value).

• On the graph, the frequency is written on the vertical axis.

Interquartile range

Interquartile range = upper quartile – lower quartile

What does the interquartile range tell you?

The interquartile range shows you how widely the central half of the sample is spread. A low interquartile range shows that the data are closely grouped together, whereas a higher figure reflects wider differences between the data (also called a wider spread).

Percentiles

Percentiles divide the data into hundredths. The median is at the 50th percentile, the lower quartile is at the 25th percentile, and the upper quartile is at the 75th percentile. To find any percentile, take this percentage of the total sample, and draw across to the graph line and then down, as for the median.

Example 10.5

A test was given to 72 students. Their marks, out of 70, are summarised in the table below.

Mark	0–10	11–20	21–30	31–40	41–50	51–60	61–70
Frequency	4	8	12	16	22	8	2

a) Complete the cumulative frequency table.

Mark	0–10	11–20	21–30	31–40	41–50	51–60	61–70
Cumulative Frequency	4	12					

b) Draw the cumulative frequency graph for the data.

c) From your graph, estimate
i) the median and
ii) the inter-quartile range.

d) The pass mark was 45 out of 70. From your graph, estimate the percentage of students who passed the test.

e) The cumulative frequency graph for a second set of 72 students is shown. Make two comparisons between the results of the two groups.

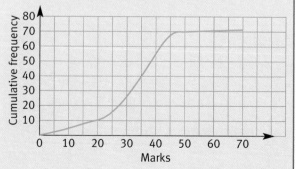

Solution

a) The missing entries are 24, 40, 62, 70, 72.

b)

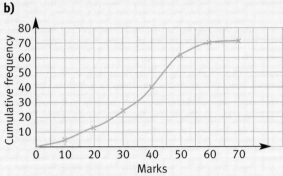

c) i) median = 38 approx. (the median is the 36th value)

   ii) interquartile range = upper quartile (54th value) – lower quartile (18th value) = 47 – 26 = 21 (approx.)

d) From the graph, 45 marks corresponds to roughly 50 people. Therefore about 22 people scored above 45 marks. $22 \div 72 \times 100 = 31\%$

e) The median in the second set of data is lower, the percentage passing is lower. (You may compare the interquartile ranges instead.)

Example 10.6

Two local sports clubs have an annual marksmanship contest. Their results for this year are as follows.

Interquartile range	Club A	10
Interquartile range	Club B	25

What do these figures tell us?

Solution

The interquartile range of Club A's results is smaller than that of Club B. This shows that their marksmanship is more consistent than that of Club B.

Note that the interquartile range does not tell you which class had the better performance – one of the measures of the average would tell you this.

Box plots

These are also called 'box and whisker plots'. These are used to show information about a set of data, in the form of a diagram. A box plot looks like this.

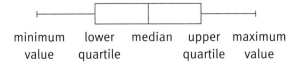

minimum | lower | median | upper | maximum
value | quartile | | quartile | value

Example 10.7

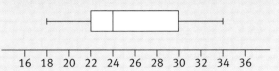

For the box plot shown above, find:

a) the median

b) the range

c) the interquartile range.

Solution

a) median = 24

b) range = 34 – 18 = 16

c) interquartile range = 30 – 22 = 8

Example 10.8

Tom and Daniel compare the number of goals they scored last term. The distributions of their scores are shown below:

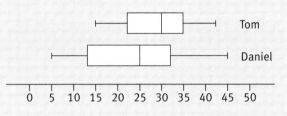

Give two comparisons between the scores of the two.

Solution

a) Tom has a higher median.

b) Daniel has a larger interquartile range.

You could compare the ranges instead of comparing interquartile ranges.

Exercise 10.4

The number of arrows shot on target by 11 members of the school archery team are shown below.

3 6 9 12 11 7 6 8 10 9 5

a) Find the median.

b) Find the upper and lower quartiles.

c) Find the interquartile range.

d) Display the information in a box plot.

Answers 10.4

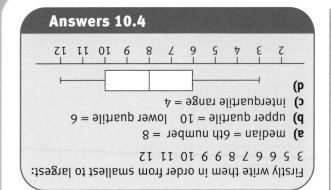

d)

c) interquartile range = 4

b) upper quartile = 10   lower quartile = 6

a) median = 6th number = 8

3 5 6 6 7 8 9 9 9 10 11 12

Firstly write them in order from smallest to largest:

Stem and leaf diagrams

Stem and leaf diagrams are used to display data without losing any of the information. They order the data, and show how the data are distributed. They can also help to find the mode and the median.

Record a mark with the tens in the stem and the units in the leaf: for example, the number 23 would have a stem of 2 and a leaf of 3; 47 would have a stem of 4 and a leaf of 7.

Start by working through the digits and arrange in a preliminary stem and leaf diagram, then reorder in a second diagram.

Example 10.9

The marks of a class in a French test, out of 50, are given below. Display the data in a stem and leaf diagram.

10, 41, 33, 27, 36, 32, 39, 21, 15, 11, 20, 31, 33, 42, 33, 25, 28

Hence find the mode and the median.

Solution

For 10, put a 1 in the stem column and 0 in the leaf column, for 41 write 4 as a stem and 1 as the leaf, etc.

Stem	Leaf
1	0 5 1
2	7 1 0 5 8
3	3 6 2 9 1 3 3
4	1 2

Then reorder the leaves:

1	0 1 5
2	0 1 5 7 8
3	1 2 3 3 3 6 9
4	1 2

The mode, the most common number, is 33.

The median is the $\frac{(n + 1)}{2}$th number.

As $n = 17$, it is the 9th number. Counting along from 0, 1, 5, 0, etc. as the 1st, 2nd, 3rd, 4th numbers, etc., the 9th number is 31.

The stem and leaf diagram in Example 10.9 shows that most of the data are grouped around the 20s and 30s, with a few numbers in the 10s and 40s. It is like a bar graph on its side.

Hints & Tips

Scatter diagrams

Two sets of data can be plotted on a set of axes. The scatter diagram shows how the data relate to each other. The **line of best fit** is a line that passes through – or close to – most of the points.

Correlation shows a link between the variables on both axes.

Positive correlation – if one variable rises the other is expected to rise.

Strong positive correlation

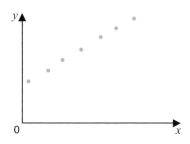

Moderate positive correlation

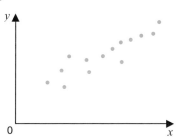

Negative correlation – if one variable goes up, the other will probably fall.

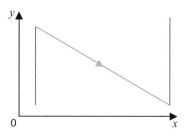

Remember **N** for negative correlation.

Strong negative correlation

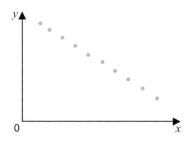

Moderate negative correlation

No linear correlation – there is no linear link between the two variables.

 TAKE A BREAK

This is another good place to take a break, before you try the rest of this chapter.

Moving averages

These are a method of showing trends. For example, the sales of an ice cream company per quarter would be quite erratic if shown on a graph, as the sales during the summer would be much higher than during the rest of the year. Moving averages graphs smooth out these seasonal changes to show general trends.

Moving averages are calculated by finding the mean of a numbers from consecutive periods.

For example, to calculate a four-quarterly moving average,

Year 1   Year 2   Year 3
1st 2nd 3rd 4th 1st 2nd 3rd 4th 1st 2nd 3rd 4th

firstly find the mean of
the first four quarters

then the mean of the 2nd
through to the 5th quarter

then the mean of the 3rd
through to the 6th quarter

Each point is plotted at the middle of the period being averaged: for example, the average of the 1st, 2nd, 3rd and 4th periods would be plotted midway between the 2nd and 3rd quarters.

For a 12-month moving average,

Year 1   Year 2
Jan Feb Mar Apr May Jun Jul Aug Sep Oct Nov Dec Jan Feb Mar Apr...

take the mean of the 1st through to the 12th month

then the 2nd through to the 13th month, etc.

Each point is plotted at the middle of the period being averaged: for example, the average of the January through to December would be plotted midway between June and July, the average of February through to January would be plotted midway between July and August, etc.

Example 10.10

The quarterly sales a small company (in £) for two years are given below.

Year 1				Year 2			
1st	2nd	3rd	4th	1st	2nd	3rd	4th
540	780	532	448	652	776	552	576

Find the four-quarterly moving averages for the given period. Display the data on a graph.

Solution

The first moving average is
$(540 + 780 + 532 + 448) \div 4 = 575$

The second moving average is
$(780 + 532 + 448 + 652) \div 4 = 603$

etc.

The moving averages are

575, 603, 602, 607, 639

Plot 575 against the point in between the 2nd and 3rd periods, 603 against the point in between the 3rd and 4th periods, etc.

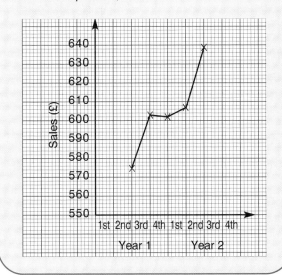

Exercise 10.5

The school concert is held every quarter. The attendance figures for two years are given below:

Year 1   Year 2
1st 2nd 3rd 4th 1st 2nd 3rd 4th
104 244 288 172 124 236 200 156

Find the four-quarterly moving averages for the given period. Display the data on a graph.

Answers 10.5

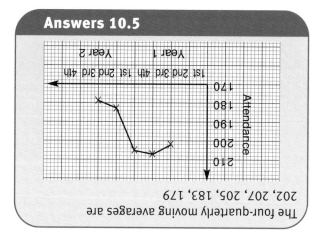

The four-quarterly moving averages are
202, 207, 205, 183, 179

Sampling

In any statistical research, it is impossible to collect data from every possible unit which may be involved. It is necessary, therefore, to take a sample which is a good cross-section of the whole.

You are often asked to comment on a sample. There are three main points to consider.

- **S**ize – is the sample big enough?
- **R**epresentativeness – are all types represented?
- **R**andomness – is the sample biased in any way?

Remember these – *if not, you'll be* **SoRRy**.

Sampling methods

Random sampling – everybody has an equal chance of being chosen

Stratified or stratified random sampling – a sample is selected according to certain criteria, but within that group the sample is random

Data definitions

Discrete – every value is separate from the next value e.g. number of cars

Continuous – every value is on a sliding scale, e.g. temperature

Qualitative – information on people's opinions

Quantitative – numerical data

Surveys

Examiners sometimes ask you to give your opinion on surveys and questionnaires. You should comment upon each of the following.

1 *The way the question is worded*

   a) ambiguous (i.e. the question could be interpreted in more than one way)

   b) leading (i.e. trying to push the interviewee into answering in a certain way)

2 *The range of responses*

   This is less common, but you should look at ways in which the interviewee can reply to see whether all possible outcomes are clearly and accurately represented.

3 *Drawing up questionnaires*

   Use the above criteria and avoid the pitfalls.

   Is the question:

   Ambiguous? **L**eading? **I**nclusive? **Bl**ased?

Remember, you always need an **ALIBI**!

Example 10.11

Students at a school carried out a survey using the following questions:

1 How often do you go to the cinema?

Never	Once a week	Once a month	Once every six months
☐	☐	☐	☐

2 Don't you think that renting a video is better value than going to the cinema?

Yes	No	Don't know
☐	☐	☐

Make a criticism of each question, and suggest an improvement.

Solution

1 The boxes are not inclusive of every answer: for example, what do you tick if you go to the cinema twice a month? A suggested improvement would be:

How many times did you go to the cinema last month?

0	1	2	3	more than 3
☐	☐	☐	☐	☐

2 By starting with 'Don't you think...', the question leads the person being surveyed into responding with 'Yes'. A suggested improvement would be:

Do you think that renting a video is better value than going to the cinema?

Yes ☐   No ☐   Don't know ☐

 TAKE A BREAK

Exam-type questions 10

1 The secretary of a tennis club drew a pie chart to show how many members had paid their club subscription. If θ is the angle representing 20 people, express, in terms of θ:
a) the angle representing 30 people
b) the angle representing the other people not already mentioned in the sample.

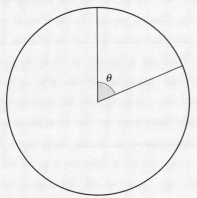

2 The table below gives the exam marks out of 40 gained by 80 pupils.

Marks (x)	Frequency	Cumulative frequency
$0 < x \leqslant 5$	0	
$5 < x \leqslant 10$	2	
$10 < x \leqslant 15$	6	
$15 < x \leqslant 20$	18	
$20 < x \leqslant 25$	20	
$25 < x \leqslant 30$	16	
$30 < x \leqslant 35$	12	
$35 < x \leqslant 40$	6	

a) Complete the table and draw the cumulative frequency curve.
b) Find approximate answers for the median, upper quartile, lower quartile and interquartile range.

c) The top 35% pass the test. Find the 65th percentile and hence the pass mark.
d) The top five people win a prize. What is the minimum mark for a prize?

3 Draw a frequency polygon to illustrate the information in question 2.
a) What is the modal class?
b) How can you tell this from the diagram?

4 Using the information in question 2, find an estimate of the mean.

5 The table below shows the time taken by contestants to complete a puzzle.

Time in minutes	0 – 5	5 – 10	10 – 20	20 – 35	35 – 40
No. of competitors	10	35	30	15	10

Complete the histogram using the above information.

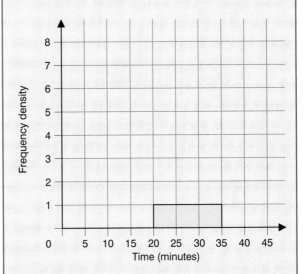

6 a) Draw the line of best fit on the diagram below.

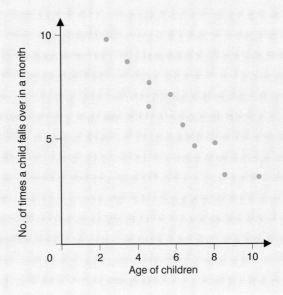

b) How would you describe the correlation in the scatter diagram?

c) Why is your line of best fit misleading when trying to predict results for babies under 2 or children over 10?

7 Do you read magazines about pop music?

Answer [Yes/No]

a) How would you improve this question?

b) Would you use a random or stratified sample when conducting a survey of this form? Justify your answer.

8 A sample was taken of the telephone calls made from a certain call box. The lengths of the calls, in minutes, are as shown on the graph below.

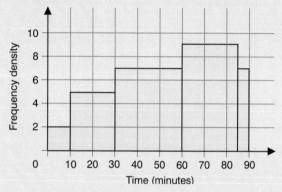

Complete the table.

Length of call (x)	Frequency
$0 < x \leq 10$	
$10 < x \leq 30$	100
$30 < x \leq 60$	
$60 < x \leq 85$	
$85 < x \leq 90$	

9 A survey was carried out on the life, in hours, of two brands of batteries A and B. The sample consisted of 40 batteries of each type. The following cumulative frequency graph illustrates the performance of one brand.

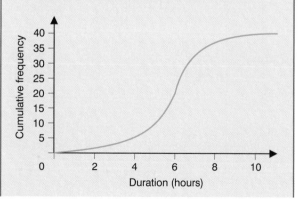

The results for the other brand are as follows.

Life in hours (x)	Frequency
$0 < x \leq 2$	4
$2 < x \leq 4$	7
$4 < x \leq 6$	9
$6 < x \leq 8$	14
$8 < x \leq 10$	6

a) On the graph given, draw the cumulative frequency graph using this data.

b) If B has the smaller interquartile range, label the graphs as A and B.

c) Which brand is better value? Give a reason for your choice.

Answers

b) The modal class is the one with the highest frequency, $20 < x \leq 25$

a) 20 – 25

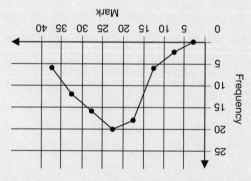

3

d) 36

c) $0.65 \times 80 = 52$nd person, graph gives 65th percentile = 27

b) median = 23, upper quartile = 29, lower quartile = 18, IQR = 11

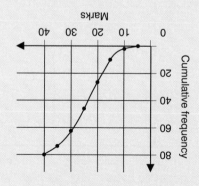

2 a) 0, 2, 8, 26, 46, 62, 74, 80

1 a) 1.5θ (not $\theta + 10$)   b) $360 - 2.5\theta$

How much have you learnt?
Tick off each topic in the list when you are confident that you can cope with it.

- ☐ **Calculate or evaluate the mean, median and mode of a set of data.**
- ☐ **Find the range of a set of data.**
- ☐ **Find the quartiles and percentiles of a range of data.**
- ☐ **Find the mean from a grouped frequency.**
- ☐ **Draw bar charts and histograms.**
- ☐ **Find and interpret frequency density.**
- ☐ **Draw and interpret pie charts.**
- ☐ **Draw a frequency polygon.**
- ☐ **Complete a cumulative frequency chart.**
- ☐ **Calculate the cumulative frequency for a set of data.**
- ☐ **Find the median from a cumulative frequency.**
- ☐ **Identify and use the interquartile range.**
- ☐ **Draw a box plot.**
- ☐ **Calculate moving averages.**
- ☐ **Draw and interpret scatter diagrams.**
- ☐ **Evaluate sampling methods.**
- ☐ **Define data as discrete, continuous, quantitative or qualitative.**
- ☐ **Evaluate methods of collecting data.**

4   $1910 \div 80 = 23.9$ (to 1 d.p.)

5

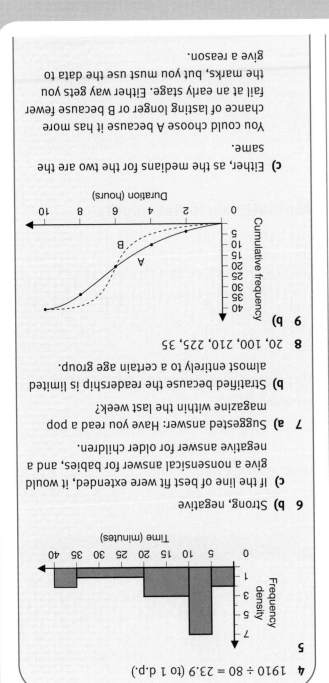

6   b) Strong, negative

c) If the line of best fit were extended, it would give a nonsensical answer for babies, and a negative answer for older children.

7   a) Suggested answer: Have you read a pop magazine within the last week?

b) Stratified because the readership is limited almost entirely to a certain age group.

8   20, 100, 210, 225, 35

9   b)

c) Either, as the medians for the two are the same.
You could choose A because it has more chance of lasting longer or B because fewer fail at an early stage. Either way gets you the marks, but you must use the data to give a reason.

Rules of probability

1 Each event's outcome can be assessed on a sliding scale, from impossible to certain.

2 Impossible events have a probability of 0.

3 Certain events have a probability of 1.

4 All other possibilities are expressed as a fraction, decimal or percentage.

5 When all possible outcomes are added together, the total must be 1.

6 The probability of an event not occurring is one minus the probability that it does occur.

Calculating probability

$$\text{probability} = \frac{\text{number of required outcomes}}{\text{number of possible outcomes}}$$

Independent events

If two events are independent, the outcome of one does not affect the outcome of the other.

The probability of both independent events happening is the product of the probabilities of each of the two events.

Example 11.1

A magician asks people to pick out two cards from a full pack with replacement (i.e. once a card is picked, it is returned to the pack). What is the probability of picking two red cards?

Solution

The combinations are:

1st card	2nd card
R	R
R	B
B	R
B	B

The probability of drawing a red card first time = $\frac{1}{2}$.

If you want two reds, you want a red AND another red. The events are independent, so you multiply the individual probabilities:

$\frac{1}{2} \times \frac{1}{2} = \frac{1}{4}$

Mutually exclusive events

These are events that cannot occur at the same time. For example, night and day are mutually exclusive because they never occur at the same time.

If the events are mutually exclusive you can use 'ADORE' (ADD = OR), but when they are not mutually exclusive you cannot.

Expected frequency and relative probability

Expected frequency = number of trials × relative probability of event occurring

Or, in short, expected frequency = np

Remember: *expected frequency is **no p**roblem.*

Example 11.2

Some children flip a buttered piece of toast in the air, to see if the old adage is true that it always lands buttered side down.

In 200 trials, the toast lands buttered side down 122 times. Find the relative probability of the toast landing buttered side down.

Solution

Expected frequency = np

so p = expected frequency ÷ n

$p = 122 \div 200 = 0.61$

Example 11.3

Leroy is practising his tennis serve. Of the 50 times he serves the ball, 17 are aces. Find the expected number of aces he would serve in 170 attempts.

Solution

$p = 17 \div 50 = 0.34$

Expected frequency = np = $170 \times 0.34 = 57.8$

Tree diagrams

Tree diagrams start from a single point. All further branches are added to the branches coming from this point. Probabilities are usually written on the branches and descriptions of the outcome at the end of the branch.

When calculating a probability, start at the base point of the tree diagram, and follow the branches along. Where the branches meet represents 'and', so probabilities are multiplied. If you go back to the base of the tree diagram to calculate a second probability, then this is 'or', so the probabilities are added.

Example 11.4

To pass a scuba-diving course, recruits must undergo two tests. The probability of passing the first test is $\frac{3}{5}$, and the probability of passing the second test is $\frac{2}{3}$. These events are independent.

Draw a tree diagram to illustrate this.

What is the probability that a candidate taken at random:

a) passes both parts

b) fails the first but passes the second

c) passes one test, but not both?

Solution

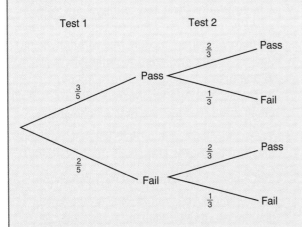

a) Reword the question as 'Find the probability of passing the first AND the second.'

$\frac{3}{5} \times \frac{2}{3} = \frac{6}{15} = \frac{2}{5}$

b) Reword the question as 'fails the first AND passes the second'.

$\frac{2}{5} \times \frac{2}{3} = \frac{4}{15}$

c) Reword as '(fails the first AND passes the second) OR (passes the first AND fails the second)'.

$\frac{2}{5} \times \frac{2}{3} + \frac{3}{5} \times \frac{1}{3} = \frac{4}{15} + \frac{3}{15}$

$= \frac{7}{15}$

Probability without replacement

Example 11.5

A riding school owns three brown horses, two black horses and four grey horses. Two members go into the stables and bring out the first two horses they find.

a) Draw a tree diagram to illustrate all possible outcomes.

b) Find the probability that both horses are brown.

c) What is the probability that both horses are of the same colour?

d) What is the probability that both horses are of different colours?

Solution

a) Method for drawing the tree diagram:

   i) The first person has 9 horses to choose from, so the second person has 8. Fill in all the denominators first.

   ii) The numerators for the first horse chosen are simple – they are the numbers given.

   iii) Look at each second stage in turn – e.g. if a brown horse was chosen first, there are two brown left but the others remain unchanged.

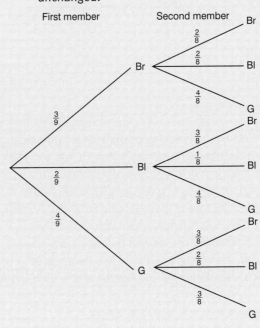

b) The question can be reworded as 'a brown first AND a brown second'.

The probability that the first horse is brown is $\frac{3}{9}$. (Do not cancel at this stage.)

You are now left with a total of eight horses, two of which are brown, so the probability that your second horse is brown is $\frac{2}{8}$.

So the probability that both are brown

$= \frac{3}{9} \times \frac{2}{8} = \frac{6}{72} = \frac{1}{12}$

(You should always cancel at the end where possible.)

c) If they are both the same colour, they could be: brown and brown or black and black or grey and grey

$\frac{3}{9} \times \frac{2}{8} + \frac{2}{9} \times \frac{1}{8} + \frac{4}{9} \times \frac{3}{8} = \frac{5}{18}$

d) If the horses are not of different colours, they must be the same colour.

P(they are of different colours)
= 1 − P(they are the same colour)
$= \frac{13}{18}$

Exercise 11.1

1 After a walk in the countryside, Mia is trying to make her way home. She is at point A and her home is at Z. At each junction A, P and Q she is equally likely to turn right or left. What is the probability that she reaches home?

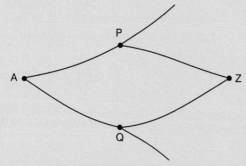

2 In a village there are three associations: the Women's Guild, which only allows women as members, the men-only Men's Club, and the church which welcomes everybody. If the probabilities of a person picked at random joining one of these groups are 0.2, 0.15 and 0.45 respectively, would you expect the probability of a person belonging to:
  a) the Women's Guild or the church to be 0.65?
  b) the Women's Guild or the Men's Club to be 0.35?
Give reasons for your answers.

3 A supermarket has Lemonade and Diet Lemonade on special offer, but the bottles are mixed up and unlabelled. At the end of the week, they have six bottles of Lemonade and four of Diet Lemonade left. If two people then buy one bottle each, find the probability that:
  a) both bottles are ordinary Lemonade
  b) one bottle of each is sold.

4 A child rolled a die 90 times and recorded the results.

Score	1	2	3	4	5	6
Frequency	9	17	13	20	18	13

  a) Write down the relative frequency of a score of 5.
  b) If the die is unbiased, what would you expect to be the frequency of a score of 2?

5 At a fairground, a girl is given two darts to throw at a dartboard. For each bull's-eye she hits, she wins a prize. If the probability that she hits the bull's-eye with a dart is 0.3, find the probability that she:
  a) wins 2 prizes
  b) wins exactly one prize.

6 Two fair dice are thrown. The smaller score is subtracted from the larger score.
  a) What is the probability that the difference is zero?
  b) What is the probability that the difference is greater than 3?

7 A bag contains three red counters and four green counters. Three counters are chosen at random. Each time a counter is withdrawn it is not replaced. Calculate the probability that:
  a) the first two counters chosen are red;
  b) the second counter chosen is green;
  c) all three counters are of the same colour.

8 In a small village, the probability that a person plays for the bowls team is $\frac{1}{7}$. The probability that a person wears glasses is $\frac{3}{7}$. Why is the probability of a person playing for the bowls team or wearing glasses not necessarily $\frac{4}{7}$?

9 An apple is growing on a tree. The probability of it falling this week is 0.8. If it does not fall this week, the probability of it falling next week is 0.9.
  a) Draw a tree diagram to represent this information.
  b) i) Calculate the probability that it will fall next week.
  ii) Calculate the probability that the apple will have fallen by the end of next week.

6 Firstly set out a table of outcomes:

		First die					
		1	2	3	4	5	6
Second die	1	0	1	2	3	4	5
	2	1	0	1	2	3	4
	3	2	1	0	1	2	3
	4	3	2	1	0	1	2
	5	4	3	2	1	0	1
	6	5	4	3	2	1	0

a) $\frac{6}{36} = \frac{1}{6}$ **b)** $\frac{6}{36} = \frac{1}{6}$

7 a) Remember that after the first red counter has been taken there are two red counters out of six. $\frac{3}{7} \times \frac{2}{6} = \frac{1}{7}$

b) The first counter may be red or green:
$\frac{3}{7} \times \frac{4}{6} + \frac{4}{7} \times \frac{3}{6} = \frac{4}{7}$

c) The counters may be all red or all green:
$\frac{3}{7} \times \frac{2}{6} \times \frac{1}{5} + \frac{4}{7} \times \frac{3}{6} \times \frac{2}{5} = \frac{1}{7}$

8 The short answer is because the events may not be mutually exclusive. That is, there may be some people that are both playing for the bowls team and wearing glasses. If the probabilities are added together, these people will be double counted.

9 a)

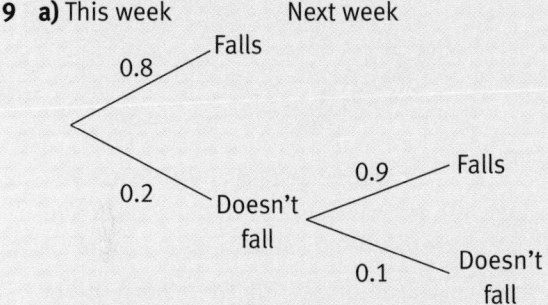

This week   Next week
        Falls
0.8
0.2
        Doesn't   0.9 Falls
        fall
                     0.1 Doesn't
                          fall

b) i) Probability that it falls next week is $0.2 \times 0.9 = 0.18$

ii) This is the probability that it falls this week or the probability that it falls next week, $0.8 + 0.18 = 0.98$

10 a)

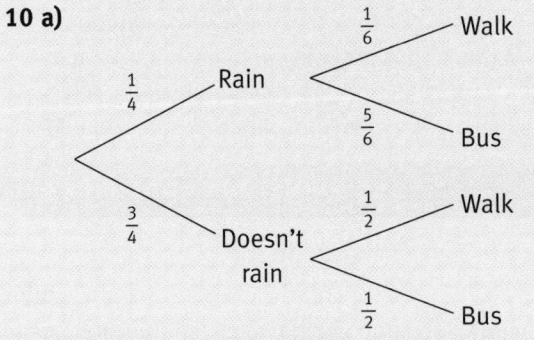

                     $\frac{1}{6}$ Walk
        Rain
$\frac{1}{4}$
                     $\frac{5}{6}$ Bus
$\frac{3}{4}$
                     $\frac{1}{2}$ Walk
        Doesn't
        rain
                     $\frac{1}{2}$ Bus

b) Start from the root of the tree diagram – there are two different ways by which he can walk.
Probability that he walks is $\frac{1}{4} \times \frac{1}{6} + \frac{3}{4} \times \frac{1}{2} = \frac{5}{12}$

---

1 She can either go APZ or AQZ, so the probability is $0.5 \times 0.5 + 0.5 \times 0.5 = 0.5$

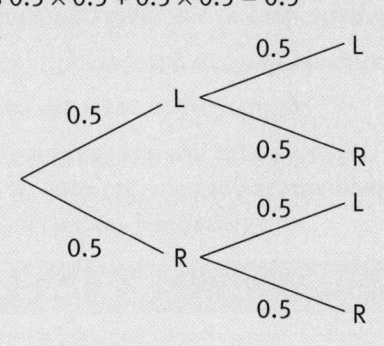

                     0.5 L
        0.5 L
                     0.5 R
        0.5 R
                     0.5 L
                     0.5 R

2 a) Not necessarily, because the events are not mutually exclusive – people can be members of both.

b) Yes, because the events are mutually exclusive – there is no overlap between the two groups.

3 a) $\frac{1}{3}$ **b)** $\frac{8}{15}$

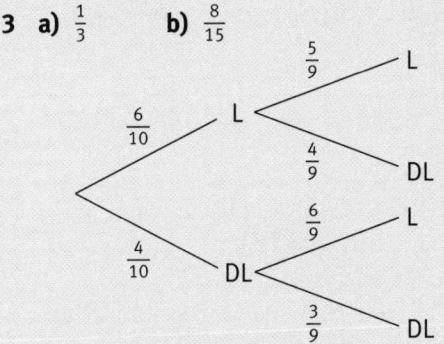

                     $\frac{5}{9}$ L
        $\frac{6}{10}$ L
                     $\frac{4}{9}$ DL
        $\frac{4}{10}$ DL
                     $\frac{6}{9}$ L
                     $\frac{3}{9}$ DL

4 a) Relative frequency $= \frac{18}{90} = \frac{1}{5}$

b) If the die is unbiased, the probability of scoring 2 would be $\frac{1}{6}$, so the expected frequency $= 90 \times \frac{1}{6} = 15$

5 a) $0.3 \times 0.3 = 0.09$

b) She may hit the bull's-eye with either the first or second dart. $0.3 \times 0.7 + 0.7 \times 0.3 = 0.42$

(This may be solved using a tree diagram.)

Answers 11.1

10 A boy either walks or takes the bus to school. If it is raining, the probability that the boy walks to school is $\frac{1}{6}$. If it is not raining, the probability that he goes by bus is $\frac{1}{2}$. If the probability of it raining on any particular day is $\frac{1}{4}$:

a) draw a tree diagram to represent this information;

b) find the probability that he walks to school.

Probability

TAKE A BREAK

Are you still with us? Take a break and congratulate yourself.

Exam-type questions 11

1. Components in a machine have a 0.7 chance of being faulty. In a batch of 3000 machines, how many would you expect to find with a faulty component?

2. A sample is divided into the following groups.
   a) men who wear glasses
   b) men without glasses
   c) women with glasses
   d) women with hats
   Which two groups are not mutually exclusive?

3. A game at a fair requires players to spin two unbiased spinners as shown below. The two numbers shown are then added.

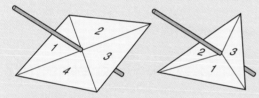

   a) List all the possible scores.
   b) What is the probability of scoring 5?
   c) What is the probability of not scoring 7?
   d) What is the probability of scoring more than 7?

4. The probability of passing a test first time was found to be 0.6. Students who took the test a second time had a failure rate of 0.3. Of those taking it a third time, 90% passed.
   a) Draw a tree diagram below, showing this information.

   b) What is the probability of passing the test on the first or second attempt?
   c) If 1000 people took the test, how many would you expect to fail at all three attempts?

5. At a school fair, three competitors throw wet sponges at a teacher. If each has a 40% chance of hitting the target, find:
   a) the probability that they all miss
   b) the probability that only one will hit the teacher
   c) the probability that the teacher will get wet.

6. Two people play a game which can either be won or lost. One player has a 0.25 chance of winning a game. If they play two games, find the probability that this player will:
   a) win two games
   b) win exactly one game.

Answers

6. b) $2 \times (0.25 \times 0.75) = 0.375$
   a) $0.25 \times 0.25 = 0.0625$

5. c) $1 - 0.216 = 0.784$
   b) $0.6 \times 0.6 \times 0.4 \times 3 = 0.432$
   a) $0.6 \times 0.6 \times 0.6 = 0.216$

4. c) 12 i.e. $0.4 \times 0.3 \times 0.1 = 0.012$ (fail and fail and fail)
   b) $0.6 + 0.4 \times 0.7 = 0.88$

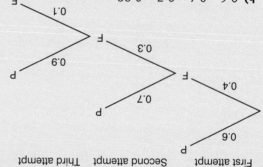

   First attempt   Second attempt   Third attempt

   a)

3. a) 2, 3, 4, 5, 6, 7 are the possible outcomes
   b) $\frac{3}{12}$ c) $\frac{4}{12} = \frac{1}{3}$ d) 0

2. c) and d)

1. 2100

REVIEW

How much have you learnt?
Tick off each topic in the list when you are confident that you can cope with it.

☐ **Use the rules of probability.**

☐ **Identify mutually exclusive events.**

☐ **Draw tree diagrams to evaluate probabilities.**

☐ **Calculate probabilities for events carried out 'without replacement'.**

Three steps to success

Here are lists of most of the topics that are commonly found on exam papers. You can also check the *Preview* at the beginning of each chapter to make sure that you've covered everything.

Step 1

These are the 'bread and butter' topics from Intermediate Level which usually come up on Higher Level exam papers. Get them right and you will have most of the marks you need for a grade C.

- Fractions, decimals, percentages and ratio
- Standard form
- Upper and lower limits
- Basic equations and expressions, simultaneous equations, simplifying and rearranging formulae
- Recognising graphs of mathematical equations
- Inequalities
- Sequences and the nth term
- Trial and improvement
- Recognising a formula as being one for a length, an area, a volume, or none of these
- Corresponding, opposite and alternate angles
- Pythagoras' theorem and SOH CAH TOA trigonometry
- Bearings
- Interior and exterior angles of polygons
- Area and circumference of circles
- Loci and constructions
- Circle theorems
- Transformations
- Mean, median, mode and range
- Stem and leaf diagrams, box plots, cumulative frequency, frequency polygons and moving averages
- Pie charts, cumulative frequency and frequency polygons
- Samples and surveys
- Basic probability

Step 2

To push that grade up to a B, you should be comfortable with these topics.

- Exponential growth and decay
- Direct and inverse proportionality
- Algebraic fractions
- Solving quadratic equations by factorising and using the quadratic formula

- Gradient and equation of a line or two perpendicular lines
- Regions and inequalities
- Recognising quadratic and cubic graphs
- Congruent triangles
- Area of non-right-angled triangles
- Sine rule
- Similar shapes, including using linear, area and volume scale factors
- Magnitude of a vector
- Histograms
- Quadratic equations including the difference of two squares and the use of the quadratic formula
- Probability without replacement

Step 3

For that A or A*, you'll need to be happy with these.

- Roots and powers without a calculator (e.g. Find the value of $32^{2/5}$)
- Surds and other irrational numbers
- Completing the square
- Sketching graphs of quadratic equations
- Recognising cubic and reciprocal graphs
- Recognising and/or sketching sin, cos and tan graphs
- Area or arc length of a sector or segment of a circle
- Vectors with boats or planes
- Cosine rule
- Functions
- Mathematical proofs
- Circle graphs of the form $x^2 + y^2 = r^2$
- Primary and secondary data
- Tree diagrams and recognising mutually exclusive events

Now see how you get on with the exam-style questions that follow. They should show up your weak spots – if any! Look back in the book to the relevant chapters to fill in the gaps.

Countdown to the exam

Exam-style questions
(use of a calculator not allowed)

1 Express $2^3 \div 2^5$

   a) as a power of 2

   b) as a fraction.

2 Two fair six-sided dice are thrown. Find the probability of:

   a) the sum of the two numbers on the dice being 10 or more

   b) both dice showing the same number

   c) both dice showing different numbers.

3 The lengths of telephone calls made by a household over the last 12 months were as follows.

Length of call (t minutes)	Frequency
$0 < t \leqslant 5$	40
$5 < t \leqslant 10$	30
$10 < t \leqslant 20$	70
$20 < t \leqslant 40$	60
$40 < t \leqslant 80$	80

   a) Complete the histogram on the diagram below.

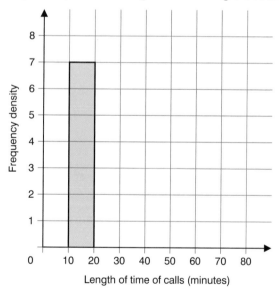

   b) What does 1 square unit on the grid represent?

4 Write as an interval approximation 4.32 corrected to 2 d.p.

5 Write an an expression for the nth term of each of the following sequences.

   a) $\frac{1}{7}, \frac{2}{11}, \frac{3}{15}, \frac{4}{19} \ldots$

   b) $\frac{7}{9}, \frac{11}{12}, \frac{15}{17}, \frac{19}{24} \ldots$

6 The diagram below shows the graph of $y = x^2 - 3x$

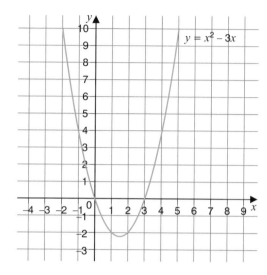

Using the graph, estimate the solutions of:

   a) $x^2 - 3x = 5$

   b) $x^2 - 4x - 2 = 0$

7 Using the axes below, draw the graph of $y = x^2 - 4x + 2$

   a) From your graph, estimate the solutions of $x^2 - 4x = -2$

   b) By drawing a suitable line, find approximate values of x for which $x^2 - 4x + 2 = x + 3$

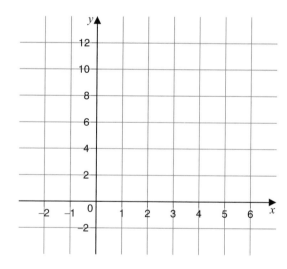

8 The speed of light is approximately 3×10^8 m/s. Find the time light takes to travel 6.3×10^6 km.

9 a) Solve the following equations.

     $2x - 5y = 20$

     $3x - 4y = 23$

   b) Find x where $7 - 8x = x + 2$, expressing your answer as a fraction.

118

10 ABCD is a cyclic quadrilateral in the circle centre O. XY is a tangent to the circle at C. Angle BCY = 37°. Angle DBC = 42°. Find:
a) angle CDB   **b)** angle DAB.

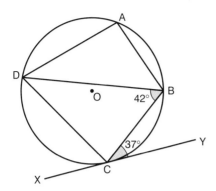

11 On the diagram below, indicate the required region such that:
$4x + 3y \leqslant 24$ $2x + 3y \leqslant 18$ $x \geqslant 2$ $y \geqslant 1$

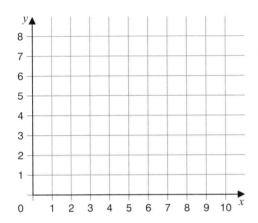

12 a) Using the diagram below, write an expression for AC^2.

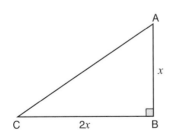

b) If $AC^2 = 20$, find the lengths of the other two sides. Show your working.

13 Find the values of x which satisfy the following equation.

$$2x - 1 = \frac{3}{x}$$

14 a) Find the gradient of the line $5x - 4y = 3$.
b) Give the equation of the line parallel to $5x - 4y = 3$ which passes through the point $(1, -2)$.

15 a) Find the set of values for x which satisfy the following inequalities.

$$4x + 1 < 39 \qquad \frac{x}{6} \geqslant 1.2$$

b) Find the largest integer value of x that satisfies these requirements.

16 Draw a line AB of length 7 cm. Showing all construction lines, draw:
a) its perpendicular bisector
b) the locus of the point C where angle ACB is always 90°.

17 a) Factorise fully the following expression.
$4\pi r^2 h - 16\pi r^2 h^2$
b) i) Factorise fully the expression $25x^2 - 1$.
     ii) Hence express $\dfrac{5x + 1}{25x^2 - 1}$ in its simplest form.

18 y is related to x by the formula $y = ab^x$, where a and b are constants. If the graph of the equation passes through the points $(0, 2)$ and $(-1, \frac{1}{2})$, find the value of a and b.

19 The graph of $y = f(x)$ is shown below. On the same axes, draw the graph of:
a) $y = f(x + 2)$
b) $y = f(\frac{1}{2}x)$.

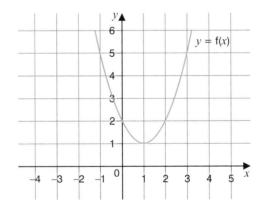

20 What straight-line graph could be drawn on the graph of the equation $y = x^2 - x$ to solve the equation $x^2 - 3x + 4 = 0$?

21 Write $\sqrt{\dfrac{3xy}{27x^5}}$ in the form $a^{-1}x^b y^c$, stating the values of a, b and c.

22 $-3 \leqslant x \leqslant 4$ and $-2 \leqslant y \leqslant 1$
a) What is the minimum value of xy?
b) What is the minimum value of x^2?
c) What is the maximum value of y^2?

23 Match the equations to the graphs below.

a) $y = x^3$ **b)** $y = x^2$

c) $y = \dfrac{1}{x}$ **d)** $y = -x^2$

(i)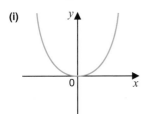

(ii)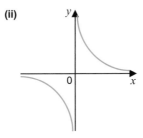

(iii)

(iv)

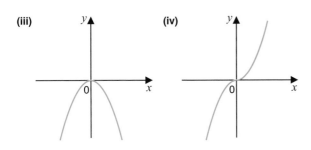

24 a) Write the expression below in completed square form.

$x^2 + 14x + 43$

b) Hence solve the equation

$x^2 + 14x + 43 = 0$

leaving your answers in surd form.

25 A solid cone has a base radius of 5 cm and a surface area of 90π cm².

a) Find its slant height.

b) Find its vertical height.

c) Find its volume, giving your answer in terms of π.

Answers

b) 10 calls

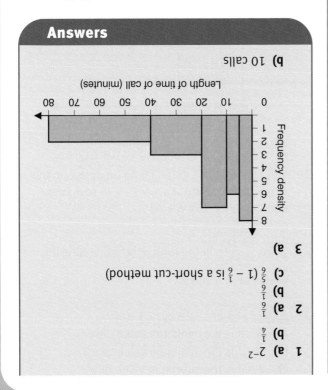

3 a)

2 a) $\dfrac{1}{6}$

b) $\dfrac{1}{6}$

c) $\dfrac{5}{6}$ ($1 - \dfrac{1}{6}$ is a short-cut method)

1 a) 2^{-2}

b) $\dfrac{1}{4}$

---

15 a) $7.2 \leqslant x < 9.5$

b) 9

14 a) 1.25

b) $5x - 4y = 13$

Hint: multiply both sides by x.

13 1.5, -1

12 a) $AC^2 = 5x^2$ because $(2x)^2 = 4x^2$

b) $AB = 2$, $BC = 4$

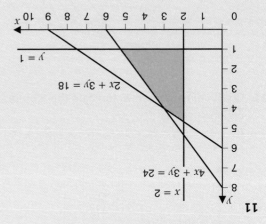

11

b) 79° (opposite angles of a cyclic quadrilateral = 180°)

10 a) 37° (alternate segment theorem)

9 a) $x = 5$, $y = -2$

b) $\dfrac{5}{6}$

8 21 seconds

Hint: convert km to metres.

b) $x = -0.2$ and 5.2

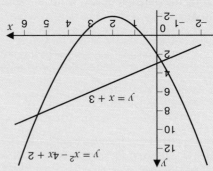

7 a) $x = 0.6$ and 3.4

Hint: $x^2 - 3x - x - 2 = 0$, $x^2 - 3x + 2$

b) 4.4, -0.4

6 a) 4.2, -1.2

5 a) $\dfrac{n}{4n + 3}$

b) $\dfrac{4n + 3}{n^2 + 8}$

4 4.315, 4.325

19

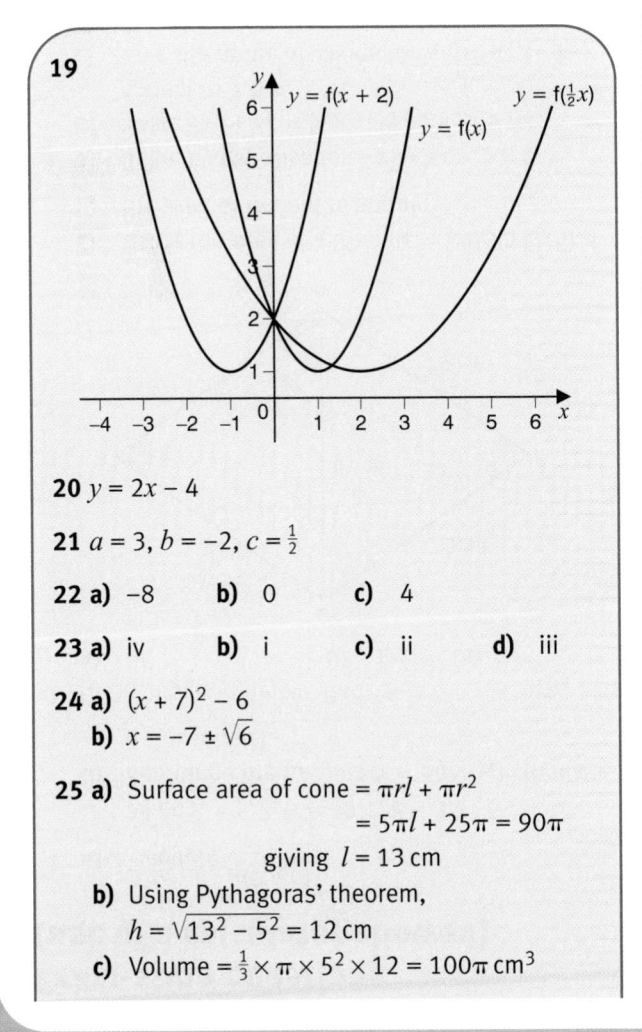

y = f(x + 2)   y = f(½x)
y = f(x)

20 $y = 2x - 4$

21 $a = 3, b = -2, c = \frac{1}{2}$

22 a) −8   **b)** 0   **c)** 4

23 a) iv   **b)** i   **c)** ii   **d)** iii

24 a) $(x + 7)^2 - 6$
  b) $x = -7 \pm \sqrt{6}$

25 a) Surface area of cone = $\pi r l + \pi r^2$
                    $= 5\pi l + 25\pi = 90\pi$
                 giving $l = 13$ cm
  b) Using Pythagoras' theorem,
      $h = \sqrt{13^2 - 5^2} = 12$ cm
  c) Volume $= \frac{1}{3} \times \pi \times 5^2 \times 12 = 100\pi$ cm³

16 a)

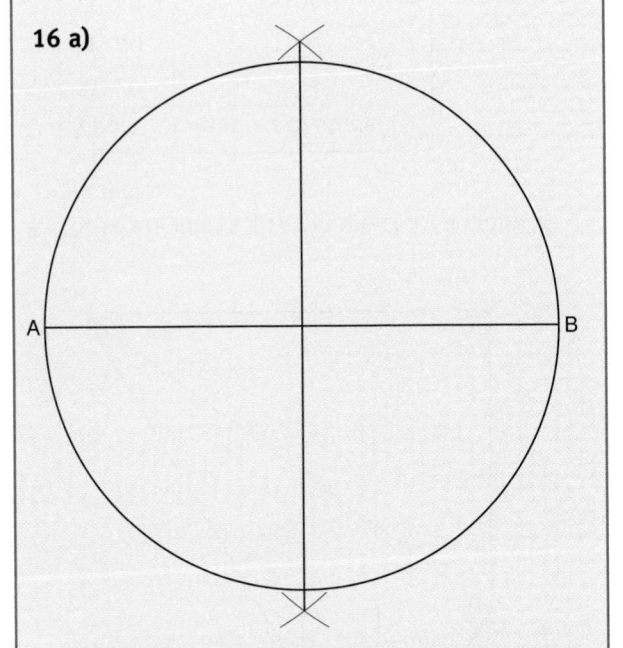

A   B

  b) The locus is a circle of radius 3.5 cm with
      AB as its diameter. (Angle ACB forms a right
      angle on the circumference.)

17 a) $4\pi r^2 h(1 - 4h)$
  b) i) $(5x + 1)(5x - 1)$
     ii) $\dfrac{1}{5x - 1}$

18 $a = 2, b = 4$

Countdown to the exam

Exam-style questions (use of a calculator allowed)

1 a) Evaluate $\dfrac{a(b + c)}{a^2 - c}$
when $a = 5.2$, $b = -0.1$, $c = 3.7$
  b) Rearrange the formula $R = 3(p - q)^2$ to make q the subject.

2 In the diagram below, find:
  a) BC   **b)** angle CDA.

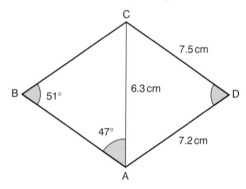

  c) Using the area of a triangle $= \frac{1}{2}ab \sin C$, find the area of the entire shape.

3 a) Solve by factorisation $2x^2 + 9x - 5 = 0$
  b) Solve $3x^2 + 8x = 5$, giving your answers correct to 2 d.p.
  c) Give the range of values for which $x^2 \leqslant 4$
  d) Give the range of values for which $x^2 \geqslant 1$

4 Two cylinders are similar. The larger holds $152\,\text{cm}^3$ and the smaller holds $42\,\text{cm}^3$. If the height of the larger is 25 cm, find the height of the smaller.

5 On the diagram below, sketch the graph of $y = \cos x$.

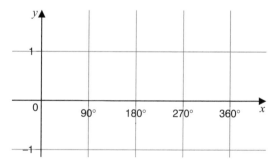

Hence or otherwise find two values of x, in the range $0° \leqslant x < 360°$, such that $\cos x = -0.5$

6 In a bag of 17 marbles, 8 are blue and the rest are green. Two marbles are drawn from the bag without replacement.
  a) Draw a tree diagram to illustrate this information.
  b) What is the probability of the marbles being of different colours?
  c) What is the probability that the marbles are of the same colour?

7 In the diagram below, find:
  a) the length OQ correct to one decimal place
  b) angle QOR to the nearest degree.

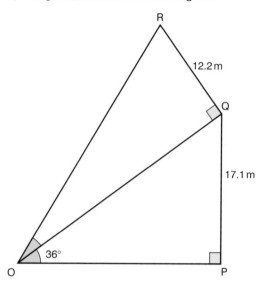

8 These are marks given in a test for a group of students.

Marks	Number of students
0–20	4
21–40	44
41–60	100
61–80	30
81–100	22

  a) Illustrate this on the cumulative frequency diagram below.

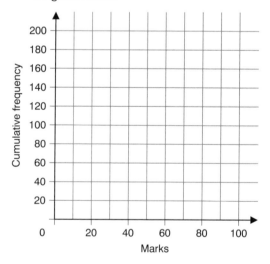

  b) From your diagram, find the median mark and the interquartile range.
  c) A student was told that she was at the 80th percentile. What mark did she obtain?
  d) What percentage of students scored above 70 marks?

9 A river is 50 m wide. The current is flowing at 0.15 m/s in a direction parallel to the bank. A woman at P can swim at 0.4 m/s in still water. She is continually aiming in a direction perpendicular to the bank.

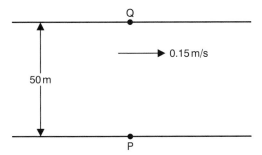

a) How far downstream of Q will she land?

b) Find her resultant speed.

10 If the height of a piece of paper was given as 11 cm and the area as 88 cm², both measurements given correct to the nearest whole number, find:

a) the maximum width

b) the minimum width.

11 Find two values of x in the range $0° \leqslant x < 360°$ such that $\tan x = \sqrt{3}$.

12 A man and a woman each invested money in a bank for ten years at a fixed rate of interest of 8.5%.

a) The woman invested £1400.00. How much was this worth at the end of the ten years?

b) The man received £6873.39. How much was his initial investment?

13 Two similar objects have volumes 6062 cm³ and 2458 cm³ respectively. If the surface area of the larger is 1208 cm², find the surface area of the smaller.

14 If you wanted to find out the attitude of a school population to the policy on school uniform, how would you choose a stratified random sample?

15 A sequence is given as 1, 5, 9, 13, ...

a) Find the 16th term of the sequence.

b) Find a formula for the nth term of the sequence.

16 The dimensions of a swimming pool are shown below.

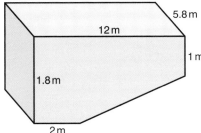

a) Calculate the volume of the pool in cubic metres.

b) Given that 1000 cm³ = 1 litre, convert your answer to a) to litres, giving your answer in standard form.

17 What is the distance from the origin to the point with coordinates (3, 4, 7)?

18 y is inversely proportional to the square root of x. If $y = 65.7$ when $x = 2.8$, find:

a) y when $x = 3.9$ b) x when $y = 52.6$

19 1 litre of orange juice is poured into cylindrical glasses of base radius 2.8 cm and height 71 mm. How many glasses will be filled?

20 In the triangle below, which is not drawn to scale, use an algebraic method to find the value of x.

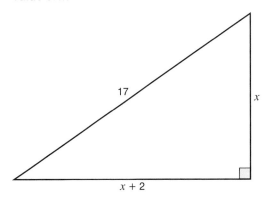

21 The numbers of occupants per car in a survey conducted over a Saturday and a Sunday were as noted in the table below.

No. of people	1	2	3	4	5
Saturday	36	30	24	7	3
Sunday	20	25	30	17	8

a) Which day had the higher mean number of occupants?

b) Which day had the greater modal number of occupants?

22 Evaluate $\dfrac{1}{p-q}$ where $p = \dfrac{1}{4.21}$ and $q = \dfrac{1}{6.84}$

Give your answer:

i) to 3 sig. figs.   ii) to 2 d.p.

23 The mass of the Earth is given as 5.98×10^{24} kg and the mass of Mars as 6.57×10^{23} kg.

a) Express the mass of the Earth as a percentage of the mass of Mars.

b) If the mass of Venus is given as 4.87×10^{24} kg, find the ratio of the mass of the Earth to that of Venus in the form $k:1$. Give your answer correct to 3 sig. figs.

24 The quarterly sales for a tulip bulb producer, in thousands of bulbs, is given below.

Year 1				Year 2			
1st	2nd	3rd	4th	1st	2nd	3rd	4th
124	88	60	44	148	92	52	28

Find the four-quarterly moving averages for the given period, giving your answers in thousands of bulbs.

25 The frustum of a cone has a height of 2 m. If the radii of the top and base of the frustum are 6 m and 9 m respectively, find
 a) its volume   **b)** its surface area.
Give your answer to 3 significant figures.

Answers

1 a) 0.802
  b) $q = p - \sqrt{\dfrac{R}{3}}$

2 a) 5.9 cm   **b)** 50.7°   **c)** 39.3 cm²

3 a) $x = -5$ and $x = \frac{1}{2}$ as it factorises to $(2x - 1)(x + 5)$
  b) $x = -3.19$ and 0.52
    Start by rearranging to give $3x^2 + 8x - 5 = 0$
  c) $-2 \leqslant x \leqslant 2$
  d) $x \leqslant -1, x \geqslant 1$

4 16.3 cm

5

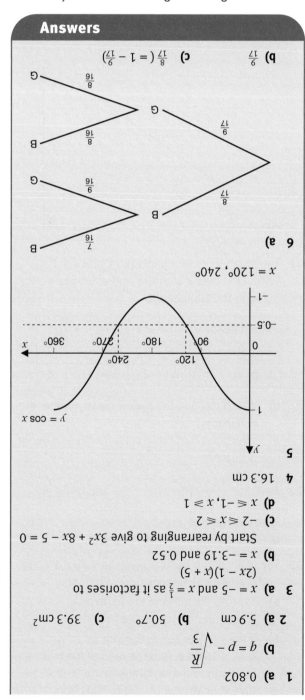

$y = \cos x$

$x = 120°, 240°$

6 a)

b) $\frac{9}{17}$ **c)** $\frac{8}{17} \left(= 1 - \frac{9}{17}\right)$

7 a) 29.1 m
  b) 23°

8 a)

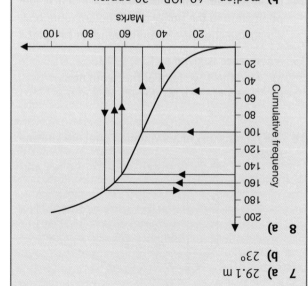

Cumulative frequency

  b) median = 49, IQR = 20 approx.
  c) 67 approx.
  d) 16% approx.

9 a) 18.75 m

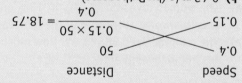

Speed	Distance
0.4	50
0.15	0.4

$\dfrac{0.15 \times 50}{0.4} = 18.75$

  b) 0.43 m/s (by Pythagoras)

10 a) 8.43 cm   **b)** 7.61 cm

11 $x = 60°, 240°$

12 a) £31165.38   **b)** £3040

13 662 cm² (Volume scale factor = 0.405, area scale factor = 0.548)

14 Separate school into year groups, and take a percentage from each group which reflects the overall membership of the school.

15 a) 61   **b)** $4n - 3$

16 a) The vertical cross-section has an area of 17.6 m² and a volume of 102.1 m³.
  b) 102.1 m³ = 1.021×10^5 litres

17 8.6 (Use Pythagoras' theorem.)

18 a) 55.7   **b)** 4.4

19 5 (Although the answer is 5.7, only 5 glasses can be completely filled.)

20 $x = 11$ (2 s.f.)

21 a) Sunday mean = 2.68, Saturday mean = 2.11
  b) Sunday mode = 3, Saturday mode = 1

124

22 a) 10.9
  b) 10.95

23 a) 910%
  b) 1.23 : 1

24 79, 85, 86, 84, 80

25 a) Using similar triangles, the height of the cone that has been removed is 4 m.
Volume of larger cone
$= \frac{1}{3} \times \pi \times 9^2 \times 6 = 508.9\,m^3$
Volume of smaller cone
$= \frac{1}{3} \times \pi \times 6^2 \times 4 = 150.8\,m^3$
Volume of frustum $= 358\,m^3$

  b) Slant height of larger cone
$= \sqrt{9^2 + 6^2} = 10.8\,m$

Slant height of smaller cone
$= \sqrt{6^2 + 4^2} = 7.2\,m$

Curved surface area of larger cone
$= \pi \times 9 \times 10.8 = 305.4\,m^2$

Curved surface area of smaller cone
$= \pi \times 6 \times 7.2 = 135.7\,m^2$

Curved surface area of frustum $= 169.7\,m^2$

Area of top $= 113.1\,m^2$

Area of base $= 254.5\,m^2$

Total surface area $= 537\,m^2$

Glossary

This is a list of the usual mathematical words that you will need for the Higher syllabus, plus some of the jargon that examiners tend to use. Questions are much easier to answer if you can understand what they are asking you to do!

arc of a circle   The length between two points marked on the circumference of a circle is an arc. The larger length is a **major arc** and the smaller a **minor arc**.

bisect   Cut in half.

coefficient   The fixed number in front of a variable. The coefficient of $3y$ is 3, the coefficient of $12ab$ is 12.

compound interest   When interest has been added to the original amount, then the interest on the new amount is found, and so on. (Alternatively, use the multiplier method, see Chapter 2).

congruent shapes   Shapes that are identical in size and shape. (Be careful to distinguish between congruent and **similar**.)

constant   A number which does not change in value. For example, in the expression $x^2 + 3x + 5$, the constant is 5. If you are drawing a graph to show $y = x^2 + 3x + 5$, you would substitute different values for x, but you would always finish by adding 5.

correlation   A relationship between two or more variables. Plot the coordinates showing the relationship on a graph. If the result is a straight line sloping up, the correlation is **positive**, if sloping down it is **negative**. If you cannot see a pattern resembling a straight line, there is **no linear** correlation.

cross-section   A 'slice' from a prism.

denominator   The bottom number of a fraction.

depreciates   Loses value.

equivalent fractions   Two or more fractions which are worth the same amount.

evaluate   Find the value of.

expand   This usually refers to brackets. To expand brackets means to multiply them out.

expression   This is a formula. If, for example, a boy is three years older than his sister, who is n years old, then the boy's age is $n + 3$. Do not confuse an expression with an equation. If you are told $n + 3 = 10$, this is an equation and you can solve it to find the value of n.

factor   A whole number that divides into another number exactly.

hence   If you see this word in a question, it implies that some information which you have already worked out could be useful in helping you to discover the answer. Sometimes you will see 'hence or otherwise'. This means that although you could use the information from an earlier part of the question, you could also use another method to find the answer.

hexagon   Any two-dimensional six-sided shape.

highest common factor (HCF)   The largest factor that two or more numbers have in common. For example, 6 is the HCF of 12 and 18.

histogram   A bar chart in which the area represents the frequency.

improper fraction   A fraction in which the numerator is larger than the denominator. You may see this called a 'top-heavy' fraction.

independent events   The outcome of one event does not affect the outcome of the other(s).

index (plural indices)   In the number 4^3, for instance, 3 is the index, or power. Make sure of the rules governing indices by checking up in Chapter 1.

inequality   Any value that is larger ($>$) or smaller ($<$) than another value. If the inequality sign has an extra line, e.g. $\geqslant$ or $\leqslant$, it means greater than or equal to/less than or equal to another value. If you have to draw the equation of a line and then indicate the region that is greater than or less than the equation, simply shade the area above (A$\geqslant$OVE)or below (B$\leqslant$LOW) the line. If illustrating a range of values on a number line, remember that the circle at each end of the line is open if the inequality is $>$ or $<$ and closed if the inequality includes 'or equal to', i.e. $\geqslant$ or $\leqslant$

integer   Any whole number, including negative numbers and zero.

inverse   A reverse process that 'undoes' an operation. Addition and subtraction are inverses, as are multiplication and division. Inverse sin, cos, tan ($\sin^{-1}$, $\cos^{-1}$, $\tan^{-1}$) are used in trigonometry to find angles when you know two sides of a right-angled triangle. Use the INV, SHIFT or 2ndF button on your calculator.

line segment   In theory, any line goes on for ever with no beginning or ending, so the part referred to is a line segment.

locus (plural loci)   The locus of a point is the path taken by the point following a given rule. For instance, the locus of a point P which is always 3 cm from a fixed point O is a circle of radius 3 cm, centred at O.

lowest common multiple (LCM)   The smallest number into which two or more numbers will divide exactly. The LCM of 12 and 18 is 36. Finding the lowest common denominator when adding or subtracting fractions is the same as finding the LCM.

mixed number   A number comprising a whole number and a fraction. At the end of a calculation involving fractions, you often need to change an improper fraction back to a mixed number.

mutually exclusive events   Events that cannot happen together.

numerator   The top number of a fraction.

octagon   Any eight-sided, two-dimensional shape.

pentagon   Any five-sided, two-dimensional shape.

perpendicular   At right angles; for example perpendicular lines meet at right angles. The perpendicular height of a triangle is a line from an angle that meets the opposite side at right angles.

polygon   A two-dimensional, straight-sided shape. Triangles, hexagons, octagons etc. are all polygons. A **regular polygon** is a polygon in which all sides and angles are equal.

primary and secondary data   Primary data is data collected at source, e.g. a questionnaire. Secondary data is the data generated from primary data, e.g. you might decide to sort all the responses from a set of questionnaires into categories dependent on the age or sex of the members of the sample.

prime number   A number that has exactly two factors, i.e. itself and 1. The first, and only even, prime number is 2. The number 1 is not a prime number as it has only one factor, i.e. itself.

prism   A three-dimensional shape that can be cut into any number of identical slices. Each slice is called a cross-section.

quadrilateral   Any two-dimensional four-sided shape.

reciprocal   In simple terms, a number turned upside down. The reciprocal of $\frac{2}{3}$ is $\frac{3}{2}$. Your calculator has a button marked either $\frac{1}{x}$ or x^{-1}. A mathematical definition is that the reciprocal is a number by which the original number is multiplied to obtain the answer 1, e.g. 2 or 0.5 is the reciprocal of 2 and vice versa because $2 \times \frac{1}{2} = 1$.

recurring decimal (or repeating decimal)   A decimal with a pattern that recurs for ever, e.g. 0.33333 ..., 0.121212 ....

sector of a circle   A triangular 'slice' of a circle formed by two radii and the arc joining them.

segment   An area enclosed by an arc of a circle and a chord.

similar shapes   One shape is an enlargement of the other. The lengths of the sides are increased or decreased by the same scale factor or multiplier, but the angles in each are identical. (Be careful to distinguish between similar and **congruent**.)

simplify   If this refers to an expression, collect together all the terms which are of the same kind. Sometimes you will need to multiply out (expand) brackets. If it refers to a fraction, cancel the fraction.

simple interest   The interest on the original amount for the length of time given.

subtend   The points at the ends of two lines meeting at an angle are said to subtend the angle. You may meet this word in questions involving circle theorems.

surd   A number in root form, e.g. $\sqrt{2}$. You may be asked in a question on a non-calculator paper to leave your answer in surd form (e.g. the answer to the length of a side in a Pythagoras question could be $\sqrt{42}$).

term   In a sequence, each number is a term. Finding a formula for the nth term means finding a formula which would enable you to find what the term is in any specified position in the list – e.g. 4th, 18th, 75th, etc. The word is also used to describe an equation or expression: the expression $x^2 + 3x + 2$ has three terms.

terminating decimal   A decimal that terminates or finishes, e.g. 0.5, 0.007, 0.23, etc. Terminating decimals are easily turned into fractions (see Chapter 1).

tetrahedron (plural tetrahedra)   A pyramid on a triangular base, so it has four sides including the base.

theorem   A rule.

variable   A quantity that varies in size, often expressed by the letters x or y. For example, in the equation $y = 2x + 4$, x and y will vary according to the values chosen.

varies directly/indirectly   Is directly/inversely proportional to.

vertex (plural vertices)   Where two sides meet, forming an angle.

Index

Index